The Path of Compassion

BY THE SAME AUTHOR:

Golden Precepts of Esotericism
Fundamentals of the Esoteric Philosophy
Occult Glossary
Man in Evolution
The Esoteric Tradition
Questions We All Ask
Messages to Conventions
Wind of the Spirit
Studies in Occult Philosophy
The Dialogues of G. de Purucker
Fountain-Source of Occultism
The Four Sacred Seasons

The Path of Compassion

Time-honored principles of ethical and spiritual conduct

G. de PURUCKER

Excerpted from FOUNTAIN-SOURCE OF OCCULTISM

THEOSOPHICAL UNIVERSITY PRESS
PASADENA, CALIFORNIA

THEOSOPHICAL UNIVERSITY PRESS
POST OFFICE BIN C
PASADENA, CALIFORNIA 91109
1986

First Edition
Copyright © 1986 by Theosophical University Press
Originally published in *Fountain-Source of Occultism*,
© 1974 by Theosophical University Press.

All rights including the right of reproduction in whole or
in part in any form are reserved under International and
Pan American Copyright Conventions.

∞

The paper in this book meets the standards for permanence
and durability of the Council on Library Resources.

Library of Congress Catalog Card Number 86-50300
ISBN 0-911500-69-3

Manufactured in the United States of America

Contents

PREFACE / vii

I — *The Primeval Wisdom-Teaching*

Passing on the Light / 3
Spiritual Illumination vs. Psychic Illusions / 8
The Still, Small Path / 14
Pledge-Fever and the Spiritual Will / 20

II — *Discipline precedes the Mysteries*

Esoteric Discipline / 29
Meditation and Yoga / 38
The Pāramitās and the Exalted Eightfold Path / 43
The Initiatory Cycle / 54

APPENDIX / 63

Foreword and Contents
  from *Fountain-Source of Occultism*

Preface

"LIVE THE LIFE and ye shall know the doctrine" say the wise of all cultures and eras. If we were consistently to live the higher life we would experience the reality of the spiritual realms. Being in communion with one's higher self, one's inner master or guru, one is privy to its wisdom garnered through many lives of learning and evolving. Every human being is a child, a disciple, of his higher self, his inner monitor. Sooner or later he will come to realize that "living the life" means living in consonance with his noblest ideals. But how achieve this? How bridge the chasm between our aspirations and the pull of material interests that hold us in bondage?

In 1974 on the centenary of G. de Purucker's birth, Theosophical University Press published *Fountain-Source of Occultism,* a vast panorama of teaching about man and cosmos based upon *The Secret Doctrine* of H. P. Blavatsky. Preceding the philosophic discourses which form the greater part of the work, Dr. de Purucker inserted two sections he hoped would create in the reader the proper atmosphere for the doctrinal studies that would follow. Unless one approaches the temple of nature with a reverent heart, any knowledge gleaned along the way could in the end imprison the soul.

Since then, the demand for guidelines has intensified, with all types of minds seeking personal transformation by any means that will help them break through their limitations. As a result, brilliant insights are coming to the fore in several disciplines; at the same time, human nature being in the main unruly, acquisitive, and unthinking, the marketplace of ideas is a jungle of discordant claims. The hunger for experiential knowledge, whether earned or not, is proving a mixed blessing.

To answer the urgent call for guidance, for an Ariadne thread out of the labyrinth of psychic and mental confusion, we have reproduced in the present booklet these first sections of *Fountain-Source* so that the seeker may have readily to hand an inspired vision of the path before him. Time-honored rules of ethical and spiritual conduct are illumined, along with warnings against quick and easy methods. There is no shortcut to

PREFACE

wisdom, no instant enlightenment, for inner unfolding takes place only from within; it cannot be induced artificially. And while the path to the gods, to conscious awareness of and union with our inner divinity, is long and often arduous, demanding our utmost in devotion, fidelity, and perseverance, it is also "bright with joy, and lighted with the fires of the spirit."

We are sustained by the knowledge that we and the whole of humanity are linked with the Hierarchy of Compassion: the Brotherhood of advanced human beings whose lives are consecrated to quickening and nurturing the seeds of altruism in the awakening soul.

GRACE F. KNOCHE

February 27, 1986
Pasadena, California

I

The Primeval Wisdom-Teaching

The Primeval Wisdom-Teaching

Passing on the Light / 3
Spiritual Illumination vs. Psychic Illusions / 8
The Still, Small Path / 14
Pledge-Fever and the Spiritual Will / 20

PASSING ON THE LIGHT

THERE IS BUT ONE occultism, one truth. The fountain of wisdom on this earth is the Brotherhood of adepts, the spiritual heart of the world, from which streams unceasingly a flow of inspiration and enlightenment. It is the one supreme source from which have derived all the facets of truth that the religious and philosophical systems of the world contain. From there come forth not only the great sages and teachers from time to time as the guides and instructors of men, but also envoys or messengers, whether known or unknown, who work in the world for the benefit of mankind.

This fountain-source of wisdom is formed of the noblest spiritual and intellectual giants that humanity has ever produced — men who have become at one with the god within. Knowing each other they band together and thus form the great school of light and truth, the great Brotherhood. Called by various names in different ages, the higher ones are known in Buddhist countries as Dhyāni-chohans; the ancient Persians referred to the members of this solar hierarchy as Amshaspends. Jewish mystics and Qabbalists spoke of them as Bnēi 'Elohīm, Sons of the Gods; and in other countries they were called Sons of Light, or Sons of the Sun as in ancient Egypt.

Innumerable schools of occultism, all derivative from the mother-school, have existed in the past, exist presently, and will exist in the future. The Mysteries of the Greeks were one such school, as were those of the Persians and the Egyptians; the Mysteries practiced in the ancient Americas, such as among the Peruvians and the Mayas, were schools in the same sacred tradition. Both the Lamaism of Tibet and the Vedānta of Hindustan are essentially schools of occultism, although they are also systems of exoteric philosophy. The Rosicrucians of the mediaeval ages were originally a mystic theosophic and quasi-esoteric body; and the Martinists of France, existing even today, form one of the 'occultistic' schools. Then there are the so-called alchemical bodies, whether in India, Asia Minor, or in Europe, whose adherents, while possessing a modicum of spiritual aspiration, nevertheless yearn even more for powers or phenomena.

There are, moreover, in the Orient a number of quasi-occult groups, some larger, some smaller, which study in their own way the different remnants of mystical literature which past ages have brought into being in those countries. In Persia, Egypt, Syria and in parts of Turkey, similar bodies exist, often very exclusive, and usually nothing is heard of them.

All such associations, in every country and every age, do a certain good work in their way in proportion to the amount of the ancient wisdom that they teach. But such truth as they do impart is too often seen through the distorting mental prisms of those who have wandered from the fountain-source. Only as they pass on faithfully the splendor originally received from the mother-school can they rightly be called schools of occultism. It may be added that there are in the world at the present time, in every one of the great continental masses, a few — a very few — genuinely esoteric schools connected with the Brotherhood.

A few intuitive scholars have suspected the existence of esoteric teachings in the archaic Mystery schools, but these have never yet been found in a coherent body. In the different literatures of antiquity we find an allusion here, a reference there, but a reasoned and explicit series of such teachings exists only in places to which no uninitiated student has hitherto consciously penetrated.

In recording the deeper truths for later generations, the ancient sages and seers adopted the use of metaphor or figures of speech, often in fantastic and curious tales: legends, fairy stories, mythological romances. Plato, for instance, through the use of myth gave out many guarded hints regarding matters taught in the Mysteries; but because he himself knew what he was about and had received permission to do this, and did it under the cloak of metaphor, it was not a violation either of the letter or of the spirit of his oath.

It is actually by so using esoteric terms that the great teachers of past ages wrote letters to each other, and composed their books, passing them from hand to hand. Those who were initiated could understand what they read; to them it was intelligible and clear; but to the man who had not been received within the 'temple walls,' the teachings were merely speculative philosophy, or perhaps meaningless jargon.

These wisdom-teachings have come down in direct succession from sage to sage, ever since the Mysteries were first instituted among men in late Lemurian and Atlantean times — a step which became essential because mankind had lost the power of direct and conscious communion with their divine ancestors. Men were thus taught to raise the soul by an effort of the will combined with intense aspiration so that they might be brought into direct intercourse, spiritually and intellectually, with their own inner god — or with some other divinity. It was in this way that the noblest truths about man and the universe were originally perceived, and thereafter 'sung' — to use the word of the Veda — i.e. formulated into human speech.

Why is it that in practically all the ancient literatures spiritual teaching was given in the vernacular of the battlefield? The *Bhagavad-Gītā*, for instance, tells of the conflict between the opposing armies of the Kurus and the Pāndavas. In the Germanic and Scandinavian mythologies there is the constant battling between the gods and the heroes; so also in the Greek, Egyptian, Persian, and Babylonian mythologies — all are alike in this respect.

The question is easily answered: to little children we give storybooks; to those who cannot understand the meaning of peace and quiet and the enormous strength that lies in these, we talk of battle and of fighting, because there is always a victor and a vanquished. Thus in the literatures of the world secrets of mystic truths were written in the epic vein in order to meet the mental characteristics of those ages. But behind all this there were the esoteric schools° which taught truth and compassion more directly, such as did Lao-tse of China: "The way of Tao is not to strive." This is the contrary of quietism, for quietism is usually spiritual stupefaction, whereas the whole effort should be to imbody in one's life and in every fiber of one's being an active spirit of compassion for all mankind.

Just as the original esoteric bodies became the great religious and philosophical schools of the past, just so the present theosophical movement was intended to be the spiritual-intellectual nursery from which will be born the great philosophical and religious and scientific systems of future ages — indeed, the heart of the civilizations of the coming cycles.

°Every system of religio-philosophical thought has had its own term for this universal esoteric doctrine. In the Hindu scriptures of the pre-Buddhist era it is referred to as brahma-vidyā, ātma-vidyā, and gupta-vidyā, meaning, respectively, knowledge of the supreme, knowledge of self, and secret knowledge: also as rahasya, a word signifying mystery and bearing the same connotation as the mysterion of the Greeks, and the gnosis of Neoplatonism and the Gnostic schools. In Buddhism, it was and still is known under such terms as āryajñāna, noble or exalted knowledge, and bodhidharma, wisdom-law or path.

In every important age, theosophical movements in various parts of the globe have been founded. A few succeeded; most of them lived for a while, did some good, achieved a certain amount of the work that was to be done, and then failed, becoming a church, a sect, a dogmatic set of beliefs. Such periodic efforts to instill into men's hearts the ageless verities will continue throughout future time, until human beings shall have so evolved that they will welcome light when it comes, and will honor it as the most precious gift that they have.

Thus it was that in 1875 two men of buddha-like soul took upon their shoulders the challenge of making themselves karmically responsible in a sense for the sending out of a new message which, by the force of its innate vigor and the persuasive power of its truths, would induce men to think. From then on science began to have stirrings of new ideas; fresh impulses were injected into the thought-atmosphere of the world and, not least, the ideal of working toward an eventual universal brotherhood among all peoples took firm hold. The chief objective was to have these ancient spiritual principles work as a leaven in human thought, in the religious and philosophical strata and, ultimately, in the social structure itself. H. P. Blavatsky was inspired to write her masterworks, *Isis Unveiled* and *The Secret Doctrine* — not for the purpose of founding another religion, but to restate once again and in fuller measure the archaic wisdom-tradition of mankind in its more esoteric aspects. As such, she was one of the links in the serial line of teachers who come at certain stated periods for the passing on of esoteric light and truth. She came at the beginning of a new Messianic cycle and the ending of an old one, and thus was the messenger for the age to come.

This succession of teachers, the one following the other, has continued through countless centuries. There is nothing amazing about it; it is simply an illustration of one of nature's laws, that just as generation succeeds generation, and one genus in evolutionary time comes after some other genus, so is there a chain of wise men continuing the flow of truth down the ages. In Sanskrit writings this is called the guruparamparā, of which there are two kinds: first, those sages who rise one above the other, as it were, in progressively greater wisdom and spiritual dignity; and second, those who follow each other in time, and in one line of succession in the outer world of men.

The same pattern was known to the Greek poets and philosophers, Homer and Hesiod both speaking of the Golden Chain connecting Olympus and earth, and later Greek mystical writers referred to it as the Hermetic Chain. This passing on of the torch of light from hand to hand has always been, and always will be — as long as the call comes from the hearts of men. When that call dies, the chain of succession remains intact, but the teachers no longer work openly.

The guardians of mankind — name them as you will, masters, mahatmas, adepts or elder brothers of the race — work wherever they see the slightest chance to do good, to cultivate the spiritual nature of their fellow human beings. Obviously, any society or group of people, or any individual, who tries to follow a noble pathway in life will receive their help, if worthy of it. Worthiness is the test, the sole test. Whenever the right call is made, it will be answered. But any call merely for self-benefit most emphatically is not the 'right call.' The only call they recognize is that given by those whose hearts yearn for light, and whose minds seek wisdom and whose souls are swayed by compassion. And further, the call must be made solely in order to lay such wisdom and light as may be received on the altar of service to humanity. There is not a single earnest heartbeat that remains unanswered, not a single soul-aspiration to help that is not faithfully registered.

Thus is the Brotherhood of adepts the guardian and custodian of the primeval wisdom, whose members are sworn to preserve it in secrecy and in silence until someone knocks at the portals with the right knock. They in turn receive light from others higher than they; and so on forever is this theosophia — the wisdom of the gods — transmitted to men along the Golden Chain of Mercury, the interpreter.

SPIRITUAL ILLUMINATION vs. PSYCHIC ILLUSIONS

SPIRITUAL AND ASTRAL forces are at work continuously, and have been so from the very earliest ages of the earth. But there come certain times in human history when the doors between our physical world and the inner realms are partly open so that men become more receptive to these subtle influences. We are leaving an era of materialistic life and thought and are entering a more spiritual one. At the same time, the world is full of evidences of an outbreak of psychical influences, and these are always deceptive, always dangerous, because the astral realms belong to a lower range of material existence, filled with evil emanations, human and other.

Such indeed is the present period, one wherein not so much the spiritual and astral energies are quickened as that we are at the junction of two great cycles, the ending of one and the beginning of another; and, concordantly with this transition of cyclic periods, the minds of men are rapidly changing, becoming more psychically sensitive. There is great danger in this, but there is also a larger chance more quickly to progress, if man's consciousness is turned towards higher things, for this accelerated movement of change is especially potent in so far as spiritual forces are concerned.

There is nothing unique about this; it has taken place in the past. An immense effort was made at the time of the downfall of the Atlantean race — an effort which culminated in the establishment of the Mystery schools which long ages afterwards found expression in the various mystical, religious and philosophical centers of the ancient world. When we examine the world's sacred literatures, we find the oldest of them containing the fullest measure of the archaic esoteric teachings. The reason for this is that from about the time of the submersion of the last island of the Atlantean continental system — recorded by Plato as having occurred some 9000 years before his day — there has been a steady increase of materiality in the world, and a consequent and equal recession of spiritual impulses. But this cycle, as indicated, has recently come to an end. The one we are entering is a very unusual one, in that it does not belong to the so-called Messianic era which is 2,160 years long, but covers a time span of some ten to twelve thousand years.

SPIRITUAL ILLUMINATION VS. PSYCHIC ILLUSIONS

Great events are in the making, for the entire civilized world is approaching a critical point in its history. There is literally a battle proceeding between the forces of light and the forces of darkness, and it is a matter of very delicate balance as to which side of the dividing line between spiritual safety and spiritual retrogression the scales of destiny will fall.

In a letter written shortly before her death, H. P. Blavatsky warned:

Psychism, with all its allurements and all its dangers, is necessarily developing among you, and you must beware lest the Psychic outruns the Manasic and Spiritual development. Psychic capacities held perfectly under control, checked and directed by the Manasic principle, are valuable aids in development. But these capacities running riot, controlling instead of controlled, using instead of being used, lead the Student into the most dangerous delusions and the certainty of moral destruction. Watch therefore carefully this development, inevitable in your race and evolution-period, so that it may finally work for good and not for evil.°

Unfortunately, as is always the case in an age which has lost touch with spirituality, people today yearn for powers, for the development of suspected but scarcely accepted higher faculties; and in their blindness they search outside of themselves. Their hearts are hungry for answers to the enigmas of life, and so they take what they can from self-advertised teachers about how to gain and use psychical powers, and such 'teachings' are always baited with personal benefit. It is difficult to speak of these things without hurting many trusting souls who, not knowing the truth, follow what seem to them to be glimpses of a greater life than that which they have; and this accounts for the many so-called psychical and quasi-mystical movements† presently existing which, in many cases, are leading

---

°From a letter dated London, April 15, 1891 to the Fifth Annual Convention of the Theosophical Society, American Section, held at Boston, Mass., on April 26–27.

†With a three times 'very' few exceptions, all these bodies more or less hunger after the lower siddhis which H.P.B., using the Pali term iddhis, speaks of in *The Voice of the Silence* (p. 73). In India they are represented by the different schools of yoga practice.

Siddhi, from the Sanskrit verbal root *sidh,* to be fulfilled, to attain an object, means 'perfect attainment.' There are two classes of siddhis: those pertaining to the lower psychic and mental energies, and those pertaining to the intellectual, spiritual, and divine powers, both types of which are possessed by the spiritual initiate, who uses them only for the benefit of mankind and never for self. The personal name of Gautama the Buddha, Siddhārtha, means 'one who has achieved his objective.'

people away instead of toward the light emanating from their own inner god. We have to be ever watchful in these matters. The waves of the astral light are exceedingly unreliable, and thousands and thousands follow the will-o'-the-wisps of psychic light instead of the steady burning splendor of the divinity within.

The plain fact is that the West is being misled by psychical teachings which in themselves have nothing permanent in them. And those who follow these practices are, ninety-nine times out of a hundred, people of untrained spiritual and psychical fabric of character who are thus easily caught by the māyā of psychism. This does not mean that such faculties and powers are evil or are not natural parts of the human constitution; nor that they are useless. The meaning is that they are very hazardous to one without spiritual vision and the power of intellect and spiritual will to guide and control the psychical nature in which these faculties inhere.

Dangerous also are the hatha-yoga practices of a psycho-astral type, usually connected with physical posturing, etc., to which certain individuals are addicted in their attempt to gain for themselves powers of a lower kind. These practices not only can affect the mind and even dislodge it from its normal seat, thus producing insanity, but also can interfere with the proper prānic circulations of the body. Religious fanatics often go insane; and in certain sensitive instances become the so-called ecstatics, believed by the ignorant to be exemplars of a holy life merely because their skin may bleed, and their hands or feet show wounds supposed to represent the nails of the Cross. The same may be said of the fakirs and lower type of yogis of the Orient. Results can be produced which endanger both the mind and the health, as well as the life itself. In all these practices there is not a breath of spirituality.

He who enters the path with the hope of gaining powers of any kind, regarding them as something of paramount importance, is destined to failure. Indeed, he is embarking upon a very hazardous and questionable road, which at worst could lead to sorcery and black magic, and at best will bring to him only the Dead Sea fruit of disappointment. Powers as such, whether spiritual, intellectual, or psychic, will develop in due course and in a perfectly natural way as we progress, provided that we have the unflinching determination to achieve, and, above all, that our heart is forever brightened and filled with compassionate love, a love that is even now a distinguishing characteristic of the spiritual soul within.

There is immense hope and spiritual beauty in the teachings of the esoteric tradition. In them is the path along which we may evolve, but it depends upon the individual whether or not he ascends along the ray which is living and working within him. While it is true that fully to understand the deeper reaches of the philosophy requires high intellectual power and a spiritual vision, it is often very simple natures who see a great light. Light passes everywhere. We have but to open the closed doors of our personality and the light of itself will come in, and we shall then understand instinctively the most recondite secrets of nature.

Jesus the avatāra, so ill understood in the Occident, taught the same truths. Seek first the treasures of the spirit, of the kingdom of heaven, and all other things will be added — all the psychical powers and energies and faculties will fall into place naturally and safely, enlightened and guided by the spiritual sun within.

Now what are these treasures of the spirit? None other than those spiritual and intellectual faculties and energies which make us godlike in thought and deed: will power, vision, intuition, instant sympathy with all that lives. There is no reason why we human beings should not begin to use our heritage. All powers and qualities and attributes are in us, even now, but they are latent for the most part, because we have not yet learned to bring them forth. In reality, it is we ourselves in our ordinary lower mind and feelings who are 'sleeping,' whereas our higher nature is not dormant at all, but intensely active.

For instance, when the spiritual will is evoked and active in a man, he becomes supreme over himself so that he has absolute self-command, and not even the denizens of the astral world can in any wise control him. Will in action is a current of energy, which means a current of substance, precisely as electricity is both force and matter. Back of will lies desire. If the desire be pure, the will is pure. If the desire be evil, the will is evil. Back of desire lies consciousness. Therefore will originates in consciousness through desire. We desire, and instantly will awakens intelligence which directs this will, and we act — or refrain from acting, which sometimes is nobler still.

There is divine desire° which in men is called aspiration, and also

---

°The saying in the old Veda: "Desire (kāma) first arose in It" and then the world sprang into being means that Brahman, sleeping in its aeon-long pralaya, first felt stirring within, the seeds of divine desire to become. Consciousness was behind the desire; desire arose in it and brought will into being, and will acted on the sleeping atoms and produced the worlds.

its material reflection. How many of us allow our will to be directed by the egoistic and selfish impulses of the lower aspect of our desire-nature, the kāma principle! Consequently, as the human will is rooted in buddhi-manas, it is the intuition and the higher mānasic principle which should guide our human will to the nobler acts which it is in our province to do: deeds of brotherhood and of impersonal service; and this is the very nature and characteristic of the spiritual ego, the buddhi-mānasic principle in man.

Intuition expresses itself as instant vision, instant knowledge. But there is a great difference between wisdom and knowledge. Wisdom may be called the knowledge of the higher ego, the spiritual soul, and knowledge the wisdom of the personality. In each case it is a storing up in the treasury of experience of what has been learned and unlearned — a treasury that is not a chamber, small or vast, but ourself. Each experience is a modification of the understanding self; and the repository of memory is filled with the record of the ages, precisely as the personality is stamped and impressed with the karmic record of all the personalities preceding it which made it.

Wisdom, knowledge, inner power, all are faculties of the spirit, signifying the fruits of evolutionary unfolding of the inherent power of the spirit-soul. Intuition per se is spiritual wisdom and garnered knowledge, gathered in the treasure house of the spirit-soul in past lives. Instinct, on the other hand, may be called the passive side of intuition, which is the energic, the will-side, the alert and active aspect. Instinct expresses itself all through natural being: the atoms move and sing by instinct, even as man using his consciousness and will, may do likewise; but the song and movement of intuition are incomparably loftier than the song and movement of instinct. Both are functions of the consciousness, the one vegetative, automatic; the other, energic, awake.

The spirit is all-permeant, living and moving everywhere for it is universal. Spiritual clairvoyance, of which the psychical clairvoyance is but a dancing shadow, enables one to see behind all veils of illusion, to see what is transpiring on some distant star in the fields of space. It is the power to perceive the truth of things at a glance, and to know the hearts of men and understand their minds. It is the faculty of visioning with the inner eye, not so much a seeing of forms as a getting of knowledge, and because this acquiring of knowledge comes in a way that closely parallels the way of seeing with the physical eye, it is called direct vision.

SPIRITUAL ILLUMINATION VS. PSYCHIC ILLUSIONS

So it is with spiritual clairaudience, which is not the power of hearing with the physical ear (or of seeing, for sometimes sounds are seen and colors heard, there being an interrelation between sense and sense), but of listening with the ear of the spirit. The sounds that are heard with the ear of the spirit are heard in the silence and with the repose of all the senses. Such spiritual clairaudience will enable one to hear the movements of the atoms as they sing their individual hymns; to hear the growing of the grass, the unfolding of the rose — to hear it all as a symphony.

Socrates used to say to those around him that his daimon, his inner monitor, never told him what to do, but always what not to do.° This daimon was the 'voice' of the higher ego, which in great men is often very strong in its energy; and in some hypersensitive constitutions may be heard as a 'voice.' It is not really a voice (although that is its effect at times on the physical brain), but rather is an urge from within, manifesting also, perhaps, as flashes of light and inner vision.

We cannot understand ourselves and others unless we have evolved the understanding heart. The key is sympathy, and the method is to look to the divine being within. As we aspire to become more like it in every moment of our lives, light will come and we shall know truth when we find it. We shall become compassionate and strong — qualities that are the true insignia of the self-illumined man. The first lesson, then, is to seek the light of our own inner god, and trust it alone. When we follow this light and are warmed by its sublime and life-giving rays, then we shall see the same god-light in others.

By going to the fountainhead we find the clearest water, so why drink from the muddy waters hundreds of miles from the spring? If a man would know himself and the wondrous powers and faculties that are his, let him see himself in the universe around him, and study that universe as being himself. An epigram, possibly, but a true master key to wisdom, and containing the essence not only of all initiation, but of all future growth.

°There is an interesting reason why these intimations rarely are of a positive type, being almost invariably urgings to pause, to reflect, or to *not* do thus and so. When a man is in a state of indecision, his mind makes pictures which are transmitted by sympathetic vibration into the inner consciousness; and because the inner consciousness has this contact with the brain-mind, if the pictured action be wrong, the answer comes back, No.

THE STILL, SMALL PATH

ALL ESOTERIC SCHOOLS have taught as the very foundation of their being: "Man, know thyself!" It has ever been thus, and the key to this lies in many things. It lies in the study of the suffering that the knot of personality experiences before its intricate labyrinth of selfishness is overpassed; it lies also, on a more exoteric plane, in the perusal of the majestic literatures of past ages: the brain work, the heart work, the work of the soul, of the seers and sages of every era. Greatest of all, it lies in the study of love for others and utter forgetfulness of self. Therein rests the mystery of Buddhahood, of Christhood: forgetfulness of self, absorption in love all-encompassing, unbounded, frontierless, of all that is.

Some people imagine that the path of spiritual attainment is far away over the mountains of the future, almost unreachable, when in reality there is a relatively narrow frontier between ordinary life and that followed by the neophyte or chela. Essentially the difference is one of outlook, and not of metaphysical distance. It is the same difference that exists between the one who falls under the sway of temptation and thereafter becomes its bondslave, and the other who successfully resists the temptation and thereafter becomes its master.

Anyone can enter upon the path, if his will, his devotion and yearnings are directed toward being of greater service to others. The only thing that prevents him from taking that most beautiful step is his convictions, his psychological and mental prejudices which distort his perspective. We are all learners, all of us have illusions. Even the mahatmas and adepts have illusions, albeit of an extremely subtle and lofty character, which prevent them from going still higher — and this is one of the reasons they are so compassionate towards those who are seeking to tread the very path along which they have successfully advanced in former days.

The quickest way to overcome these illusions is to cut the root of them, and that root is selfishness in its multimyriad forms. Even the yearning for advancement when it is for self alone is based on selfishness which in turn produces its own subtle and powerful māyās. Therefore every ambition to succeed, unless it be washed clean of all personality, will inevitably defeat itself, for the way of inner growth is self-forgetfulness, a giving up of personal ambitions and longings of any and every kind, and a becoming an impersonal servitor of all that lives.

It should be stated, however, that the purpose of genuine occultism is not to 'produce disciples' or to turn refractory human material into individuals striving for mere self-advancement. Rather is it to regenerate our imperfect human nature into becoming at first nobly human, and finally godlike — and this along the archaic and traditional lines of teaching and discipline which have been recognized and followed for ages past.

Chelaship is a vision, out of which arise conviction and definite action. All the rules of moral conduct that one may read about in the great literatures of the ancient philosophies as well as in theosophical writings, are simply powerful aids to help the aspirant cleanse himself of selfishness. The real code of ethics is an unwritten one, and therefore not subject to dogmatisms, not easily enslaved to conventional notions or misconstruction by minds debating and quarreling about mere words. In essence it is of the extremest simplicity, for the most beautiful and the most comprehensive truths are always the simplest. There are times when I throw my pen aside and say to myself: let us have just the simple truths that the little ones with their unspoiled natures and their direct and quick perception can grasp. It is difficult permanently to deceive a child. But when it is said that the neophyte must regain the child state, this does not mean childishness or stupidity! It is the child's heart that we need — trusting, intuitive, and alert.

Intellectual training is very valuable and a great help, but to become as a 'little one' is the most difficult lesson for human beings to learn. The brain-mind is a good instrument when guided and trained, but is a tyrant when left to its own devices and impulses, for it is always selfish; its vision is necessarily limited to the swirl of the lower and restricted field of consciousness of the mānasic knot of personality. In the higher nature lies the higher understanding, and it alone can arrive at the inner meaning of the teachings. The lower mind can achieve some success in the brain-mind comprehension of them, but only when helped from the inner understanding. An individual may be quite sincere, quite willing to know, quite ready to experiment and to investigate, but the buddhic splendor may be completely absent. The only test of fitness is that which is given by the individual himself. If the light of buddhi be shining even by so much as a fugitive glimmer, that is enough. There is then in that individual the esoteric right to know.

Self-conquest is the path of growth. The whole truth is contained in these few simple words. It is a slow growth as with all great things; and if it is to be attained, it must be an unfolding of the man himself. There is no other path than that of inner development, no easy way: the one who cannot control himself in the affairs of daily life and does not know who or what he is, cannot control the events and experiences that inevitably arise around anyone who succeeds, even in small degree, in approaching that "straitest of all gates."

Here is a strange paradox: if one would be master of himself he must be utterly *selfless,* and yet he must be *himself* utterly. The lower self must be wiped out — not killed, but wiped out, which means withdrawn inwards and absorbed by the higher self. For the higher self is our essential or real being, and the lower is but a ray therefrom — soiled, rendered unclean, so to say, because it becomes attached to this world of multimyriad illusions.

The man most easily deceived is the man most infolded in māyā; and such are often the so-called worldly-wise. You cannot deceive an adept, as he would instantly see the attempt at deception; and the reason is that you cannot, as it were, throw hooks of personal attachment into his being. Nothing one can do or say will affect him or attract him to your thought if it is in the slightest degree selfish, nonuniversal. He is above those illusions, has fought through them, found them out and rejected them. Yet the masters feel, even before we ourselves would realize it, the slightest moving of the true chela spirit. The call upon them is tremendous, and a quick magnetic sympathy is thereupon established.

Taking the thought a step further: when a neophyte makes a deliberate and actual choice with all the strength of his being, he kindles a light within, and this is the buddhic splendor; and, as said, it is sensed understandingly and watched and cared for by the teachers, and thus he is an 'accepted chela.' How long will he remain such? None is picked out by perambulating magicians wandering the world, selecting whom they may think to be proper material — not at all. The choice is in the individual: he chooses his path; he makes his resolve; and if the buddhic light is seen, be it only a spark, he is accepted, although that fact may be unknown to himself for the time being. Thereafter all depends upon him, whether he succeed or fall by the wayside.

THE STILL, SMALL PATH

It is a matter of the rarest occurrence for one immediately to know that he has been accepted, for the usual rule is that he is tested in a hundred thousand different ways, these tests arising out of the ordinary events of life and the aspirant's reactions to them. Once, however, that he becomes cognizant of his teacher, the path becomes both easier and more difficult — easier because there is the new conviction that at least a certain success has been attained, and also because of the courage and self-confidence that arise out of this fact; vastly more difficult because from now on he is under more direct training and guidance, and small lapses and little backslidings, for which large indulgence is allowed in the beginning, have henceforth very serious consequences.

Moreover, no teacher makes himself known to his disciple without the latter's having previously received many instructive premonitions from his own inner being. The reason is clear: no one ever becomes accepted, until he has actually been accepted by his own inner divinity, i.e. until he has become more or less aware of the stirring within him of a wondrous mystery.

A certain stage of progress is of course necessary before such a choice can be made; but every normal being can make such a choice, because in him spirit and matter have attained a more or less stable equilibrium. In other words, chelaship may be undertaken at any stage by anyone who can arouse the Christ-light in his mind and heart. His resignation of the lower selfhood on the altar is what counts; and no human cry for help ever passes unheard, if that cry for more light be impersonal. *The test is impersonality.*

Let us not imagine, however, that, because the words renunciation and sacrifice are often used, these imply the loss of anything of value. On the contrary, instead of a loss, it is an indescribable gain. To give up the things that belittle, that make one small, petty, and mean, is to cast away our fetters and take on freedom, the richness of the inner life and, above everything else, self-conscious recognition of one's essential unity with the All.

It should be clearly understood that this training, which is one of study and of discipline arising in the spiritual and intellectual movements of the student's own soul, has never included and never will include any interference with or encroachments upon his family rights or duties. Chelaship is nothing weird, nothing queer or erratic. If it were, it would not be chelaship. It is the most natural path for us to strive to follow, for by allying ourselves with the noblest within we are allying ourselves with the spiritual forces which control and govern the universe. There is inspiration in the thought.

The neophyte's life is a very beautiful one, and grows steadily more and more so as self-forgetfulness comes into the life in ever-larger degree. It is also a very sad one at times, and the sadness arises out of his inability to forget himself. He realizes that he is very, very lonely; that his heart is yearning for companionship. In other words, the human part of him longs to lean. But it is just the absence of these weaknesses that makes the master of life: the ability to stand alone, erect and strong in all circumstances. But never think that the mahatmas are dried-up specimens of humanity, without human feelings or human sympathy. The contrary is the case. There is a far quicker life in them than in us, a far stronger and more pulsing vital flow; their sympathies are enlarged so greatly that we could not even understand them, although some day we shall. Their love encompasses all; they are impersonal and therefore are they becoming universal.

Chelaship means trying to bring out the master living in our own being, for he is there now.

There will come a time, however, if one progress far enough, when even the family duty will have to be dropped, but the circumstances then will be such that the dropping will actually be a benediction to the individual as well as to the one towards whom the duty formerly lay. Yet let no one be deceived by the dangerous doctrine that the higher a man goes, the less is he bound by the moral law. The direct converse of this is the truth; the doing of wrong to another is never right.

At no step along this sublime path is there ever exterior compulsion of any kind; only such lofty compulsion as springs forth from the aspirant's own yearning soul to advance ever farther and farther inwards and upwards forever. Each step is marked, during its earlier course, by dropping something of the personal shackles and imperfections which keep us enchained in these realms of matter. We are told with reiterated insistence that the grandest rule of life is to foster within one's own being undying compassion for all that is, thus bringing about the winning of selflessness, which in its turn enables the peregrinating monad ultimately to become the Self of the cosmic spirit without loss to the monad of its individuality.

In the above lies the secret of progress: to *be* greater one must *become* greater, to become greater one must abandon the less; to encompass a solar system in one's understanding and life one must give up, which means outgrow and surpass, the limits of the personality, of the mere human. By abandoning the lower selfhoods we pass into the larger selfhoods of selflessness. No one will progress a single step to the more expanded selfhood which already is his own higher nature, until he learns that 'living for self' means descending into still more compacted and restricted spheres, and that 'living for all that is' means an expansion of his own soul into becoming the larger life. All the mysteries of the universe lie latent within us, all its secrets are there, and all progress in esoteric knowledge and wisdom is but an unfolding of what is already within.

How little our human troubles which plague us so greatly — such a burden of sorrow — seem when we allow our minds to dwell upon these infinitely comforting realities. No wonder the Christian writer declared that not even a sparrow falleth from heaven without its being known to the divine; not even a hair of our heads but is counted and cared for. How much more so then we ourselves. Even this world of phantasmagoria and shadows is an intrinsic and inseparable part of the Boundless from which we sprang, and towards the divine heart of which we shall one day return on the wings of the experiences that we have been through, wings that will carry us over the valleys to the distant mountain peaks of the spirit.

PLEDGE-FEVER AND THE SPIRITUAL WILL

It sometimes happens that very sensitive natures when first coming in touch with the chela-path are shaken to the very core, and there is often real suffering of heart and of mind. This is all very natural. It is really the voice of the soul within that has caught a glimpse of the spiritual light, but because the brain can neither contain nor understand it, the resultant manifestation is an agony of soul. But there comes at times also, as twin sister of this interior suffering and pain, an agony of joy, an exultation so keen, that it may be even more difficult to bear.

Most of the cases where the aspirant finds himself involved in emotional or mental trials and stresses are typical of what H. P. Blavatsky has called pledge-fever. Unfortunately, few understand exactly what this is, even though many people experience it, unconsciously or only half-consciously. It can best be described as a fevered state of mind and feeling, often acting adversely on the body, and this arises out of a stirring up of the inner part of one's being, usually of the kāma-mānasic portion of the constitution.

Pledge-fever can have a noble side as well as an ignoble one. As pointed out by H.P.B.,° as soon as anyone pledges himself to give his life in service to others, "certain occult effects ensue. Of these the first is the *throwing outward* of everything latent in the nature of the man: his faults, habits, qualities, or subdued desires, whether good, bad, or indifferent. . . . You all know your earthly pedigree, but who of you has ever traced all the links of heredity, astral, psychic, and spiritual, which go to make you what you are?"

Commenting upon H.P.B.'s statement and the effect that pledge-fever has upon the earnest student, William Q. Judge wrote:†

> . . . it is a sort of heat in the whole nature which, acting like the air in a hothouse, makes all seeds, whether of good or evil sort, suddenly sprout and show themselves to the person . . .

The field in which it works is that offered by the entire being, and therefore

---

° E.S. *Instructions*, I. †"Suggestions and Aids."

PLEDGE-FEVER AND THE SPIRITUAL WILL

will include the hidden, unknown part of us which in all ordinary cases lies back awaiting other incarnations and circumstances to arise in new centuries and civilizations.

And in a further Circular issued in 1890, he added these remarks:

> Nor must it be forgotten that the taking of the pledge° brings into the field forces that help as well as forces that oppose. The appeal to the Higher Self, honestly and earnestly made, opens up a channel by which flow in all gracious influences from higher planes. New strength rewards each new effort; new courage comes with each new step forward. . . .
>
> So take courage, disciple, and hold on your way through the discouragements and the successes that beset your earliest steps on the path of probation. Do not stop to mourn over your faults; recognize them and seek to learn from each its lesson. Do not become vain of your success. So shall you gradually attain self-knowledge, and self-knowledge shall develop self-mastery.

There are many kinds of pledge-fever, but most of them are rooted in the same cause. For instance, an excessive and unwise enthusiasm without proper mental and emotional balance is a distinct kind of psycho-mental fever. Outbursts of energy, followed by severe reaction; states of mind in which the student desires to abandon everything except the one objective, to cast aside as worth nothing at all even those things which he should value as a man; the unfounded conviction that everyone else other than oneself is to blame when difficulties arise — all these are conditions of pledge-fever, a fever arising out of an over-enthusiasm with which the heart is filled and a lively sense of the responsibility that one has sincerely undertaken.

Pledge-fever is a sign of honesty; it is also a sign that the heart has been deeply touched, and the mind profoundly impressed. It means actually that the disciple is beginning to view the circumstances of his life, whatever they may be, from a radically different aspect; and further, that he is striving to burst the old bonds of selfhood. Thus it is a good sign in one way, because it shows that the nature is being stirred, that the

---

°Any vow, any pledge, it should be remembered, is taken to one's higher self, the spiritual master within, and admonitions from this source take precedence over everything. However, let us also remember that very, very few of us can claim to be in hourly communication with the god within, much less under its sublime inspiration for lengthy intervals of time.

aspirant is progressing; and anything is better than coldhearted, dead indifference, which is a spiritual and intellectual sleep.

The blank, hopeless chill and 'dead' feeling that sometimes is experienced is simply a reaction, a part of the pledge-fever cycle; precisely as a fever in the body leaves the patient for the time feeble, exhausted and cold. But pledge-fever is dangerous too, even as are the fevers which arise from nature's effort to throw out poisons from the body in order to cleanse and purify it. Far better is it if the student is able to bring back by aspiration and inflexible will the true poise and the calm confidence of invincible strength that are imperatively required. One thinks of Horace's words in one of his *Odes* (Bk. Third, III): *Justum et tenacem propositi virum* . . . , "an upright man, tenacious of his purpose" — one whose steady mind is shaken neither by the threats of tyrants, nor the thunderbolts of Jove, the clamor of mobs, nor the movements of the great sea in storm. None of these can shake him of steady and upright mind.

In dealing with these situations, one must find the division line of safety and hold to it between cultivating unwholesome emotionalisms on the one hand, and, on the other hand, turning the cold shoulder and being unsympathetic to those undergoing the fevered trials of aspiring souls who are seeking light but who, nevertheless, are still involved in the blinding veils of emotions and therefore may at any moment be in real danger of wandering from the path.

Once our feet are set upon the path, we can never go back. That is impossible; the doors have shut behind us. We can fail and either fall asleep or die, but thereafter forward we must go. When inner disturbance comes, and the fevered condition is intense, the student should use his spiritual will and draw upon the divine wisdom in the higher parts of his being. For will is an energy, and functions, as do all energies, both actively and passively. The active will is the will consciously set in motion by the directing intelligence and the innate life. The passive will is the vegetative will, those aspects which govern the automatisms of the body or mind.° Anyone can develop the spiritual will. As W. Q. Judge wrote:

°Sleep is due to the automatic action of the will, in degree at least. The circulation of the blood, the beating of the heart, and the winking of the eyelids, in fact, growth — these are ultimately derived from the automatic or vegetative part of the will, the passive side; and this acts not only in man, but in all lower things. Likewise it is the will which has been taught, through repetition after repetition, to work in grooves, properly, easily — usually unconsciously to the perceiving mind.

PLEDGE-FEVER AND THE SPIRITUAL WILL

It is developed by true unselfishness, a sincere and full desire to be guided, ruled, and assisted by the Higher Self and to do that which, and suffer or enjoy whatever, the Higher Self has in store for one by way of discipline and experience; by sinking as much as possible, day by day, little by little, the mere personal self.*

In one sense the great teacher is life itself, and the learner is he who lives each day with its varied experiences, temptations, attractions, and ups and downs of mental activity and emotional feeling. The way of meeting these tests is by equanimity, a steadiness of both mind and soul that nothing can shake; also by magnanimity, unfaltering courage, and a positive refusal to be discouraged by failure.

Whenever there is any feeling of ungoverned vaulting enthusiasm, or again of blank despair, the student should simply wait and do his utmost to regain the calm consciousness that he is a spiritual being in his inmost. For all anyone may know, his past karma may have been so noble that, like a burst of sun from behind black clouds, he may suddenly one day be illuminated, and realize that his feet are on the path.

It is a curious paradox that the outer teacher works with entire harmony and in rigid accord with the intimations arising in the neophyte's own consciousness of the presence of the inner teacher — the greatest one of all so far as he himself is concerned. Sometimes these intimations are like flashes of dazzling light breaking into his consciousness, illuminating what seems to be the dark, gloomy night of his being; and at such moments he has a realization of being on the path that is almost painful in the intensity and reality that accompany it. But these flashes of inner recognition of one's steady advance should not and, indeed, can never be mistaken for the flickerings of the brain-mind which to the unwary or unprepared are often mistaken, because of an overweening confidence and personal egoism, for signs that he already has set his feet on the path. In truth, such would-be chela is very far from it, for he has not yet attained that development of his inner nature which can withstand the temptations of daily life.

One may think perhaps that because the operations of the universe move in the silences and make no immediate and visible impression that nature may be played with. She may not be played with. Whereas a large degree of toleration — and this is the precisely exact word — is allowed

---

*"Subsidiary Papers," September 1894.

in the beginning for human failings, the rules become stricter and more rigidly enforced the farther one goes, for the aspirant has taken a holy vow of obedience to his higher self. In the more progressed stages, there is the obedience of the willing heart and of the understanding mind, for the neophyte soon comes to feel that as he becomes like unto the gods, the more necessary is it to work in harmony with nature's laws, which means obedience not to one's own conceptions but *to things as they are*. And this is the meaning of the expression that the mahatmas never will nor do they dare interfere with karma. They are the servants of the law, the obedient instruments of the supreme spiritual teacher of our globe — the Silent Watcher of humanity — and the higher the mahatma is, the more willingly and joyfully obedient he is.

It is false pity as well as an esoteric crime for any so-called teacher to mislead aspiring students by promising them anything that is not the truth of the ages: *there is no short path, no easy way;* for inner growth, inner unfolding, inner evolution, is a matter of time and, above all, of self-effort. There are moments when the truth may seem to be cold and unacceptable, but this is the fault of the neophyte and not the fault of the teacher, and only proves that the student is not yet sufficiently awakened to recognize the true from the false, the right way from the left.

It should be obvious that no master living could make a chela out of unchela-like material, for that would be like saying it is possible to set something on fire with an element that is not fire. Even were it possible to transform, by some feat of magic, an average man into a successful chela, it would be a work of the worst kind of black magic, because it would in no wise help the man, but merely make of him a created mechanism without interior strength, without interior light, without interior ability to go farther on the path. There is no attainment unless the individual makes the progress himself. Hence it is that the mahatmas will not interfere in the slow unfolding of the inner faculties of the chela's constitution; if they did, it would be an interference with growth and would lead to a crippling and a weakening of the chela, which is exactly the opposite of what is needed.°

°Everything is karmic. Whatever happens is the resultant of the many karmic energies working to find expression in a life, the strongest of these coming into manifestation first, while the less strong are not turned aside but are dammed back, to await their turn. In certain very unusual circumstances it is possible for an adept or teacher with the full consent of his pupil to prevent the appearance of the strongest

PLEDGE-FEVER AND THE SPIRITUAL WILL

The treading of the path leads to those higher spiritual and intellectual levels of consciousness whereon the masters live and have their being, but it is utterly impossible to approach them unless indeed one does just that, and breathes the rare spiritual and bracing intellectual atmosphere that they breathe. Those who would lead others should continuously remember this, for an injury is worked upon their souls if at any time they are misled by false hopes on the one hand, or, on the other hand, by the siren songs of personal ambition or the erroneous notion that the path can be followed by *leaning*. If anyone believes he can shoulder off responsibility for his thoughts and acts upon another, whether that other be a hypothetical god or demon, a human or an angel, from that moment he begins to follow the downward path. He gives up his own will to salvation, his will to achieve, his will to conquer.

How did the masters become the great and noble men they are? Through many ages by self-directed evolution. No one can succeed, can follow the path, unless his own strength is developed, unless his own inner powers and faculties are evolved, unless his own vision breaks through the veils of illusion which surround his consciousness. It is a long process, but a glorious one.

Some students have puzzled over a statement made by W. Q. Judge regarding an age limit of forty-four years beyond which "it is hard to enter through the gate"° of the inner world, and impossible for those who have only recently given thought to these matters. This is because around middle age the veils of selfhood so enshroud the inner being that the light from within cannot easily penetrate the brain-mind; and one beginning the study of esotericism at this stage finds it more difficult than if he had started thinking along these lines in youth, or better still in childhood. But exceptions to this are very numerous.

Actually there is no need for anyone to think that because he enters upon the path late in life, no progress is possible for him in the future.

---

karmic energy first, or so to smooth its action that other karmic energies or elements can appear almost simultaneously. These rare instances are always for the benefit either of the pupil or for some great and impersonal work for humanity, and can take place only in circumstances or conditions which are actually within what may be called a higher karma of the one so submitting himself to the destiny thus modified. But even here the karma so affected will find its expression just the same, and with its precisely normal condition of power and with precisely normal results.

°"Subsidiary Papers," October 1895.

Nothing can stay the imperious energy of the spiritual will, and the very fact that an individual in middle or even in advanced life is desirous of entering upon the pathway of splendor is in itself evidence that there are working through his being a will and a determination, an enthusiasm and an intuition, which themselves are proofs of the possibility, almost certainty, of the receiving of light. Coming events cast their shadows before, and so it is here, because the light is breaking through, is behind the future events, and heralds their coming.

Chelaship is exchanging the darkness of personality for the glorious sunlight of impersonality. It is a passing out of the mire of material existence, with its phantasms of thought and emotions, into the clear splendor of the inner spiritual sun, leading ultimately to a becoming-at-one with the soul of the universe. It is the age-old path that will lead the aspirant to become at one with his own spiritual essence, which means the attaining of an enormously increased range of consciousness and life. As our spiritual nature in a sense is universal, it is at once seen that chelaship is a continuous growth towards universality in thought and in feeling, a pressing forward along that wonderful path to the outermost veil of the inner confines of the universe.

Marvelous thought: we travel without advancing, we progress without any movement. We reach the heart of the universe by losing ourself in order to gain the cosmic Self seated in our inmost essence. The pathway that we travel is long and may be arduous, but it is also bright with joy, and lighted with the fires of the spirit. The 'travel' is really a changing of consciousness, a spiritual alchemy. The heart of the universe is at an infinite distance and yet is nearer than our own soul, for it is our Self.

II

Discipline precedes the Mysteries

Discipline precedes the Mysteries

Esoteric Discipline / 29
Meditation and Yoga / 38
The Pāramitās and the Exalted Eightfold Path / 43
The Initiatory Cycle / 54

ESOTERIC DISCIPLINE

COMING NOW DIRECTLY to the matter of actual discipline in esoteric training, every neophyte is taught at the outset that the first step is "to live to benefit mankind," and the second is to practice in his daily life the "six glorious virtues" or pāramitās. Until he has absolutely abandoned any desire for personal profit or gain, he is unfit even to attempt to tread the path. He must begin to live for the world; and when his soul is inflamed with this desire impersonally, he at least is ready to begin to try.

Perhaps the most important thing for the would-be aspirant to understand is that although the chela path is almost constantly represented as one of gloom, sorrow, and endless self-sacrifice, this is but a manner of phrasing the truth. Actually, it is the most joyous course of life and guide of conduct that it is possible for human beings to imagine. Still, I have often thought that the difficulties have been somewhat overemphasized for a very good reason: to prevent personally ambitious individuals from rushing in where angels fear to tread. It is well that this is so, because the dangers of all kinds which beset the untrained and half-hearted postulant for occult progress are exceedingly real, and the chances of his making a mis-step, or of having his feet befouled in the mire of his own lower nature, are so certain that the warnings given are not only humane and dictated by the highest compassion, but are likewise nicely calculated to point out the need of discipline preceding any introduction to the Mysteries.

To restate the matter more succinctly, the path of chelaship is one of ineffable happiness for those who are fit to tread it. It means a constant living in the higher part of one's nature, where not only wisdom and knowledge abide, but where there is the continuous expanding of the heart in compassion and love to include the entire universe in its enfolding comprehension. Indeed, its beauties are so sublime that a veil is almost always deliberately drawn over these so that the unwary shall not be tempted to trespass into regions whose thin and life-giving aether their lungs cannot as yet in any wise breathe. Our West has forgotten for too long a time, despite the fine ethical teachings of its accepted religion, that the life of the spirit while in the body is the only life worth while, and actually is a preparation for living self-consciously and without diminution of faculty or power beyond the portals of death.

Chelaship, therefore, is the learning to be 'at home' in realms other than the physical sphere; and it should be apparent that the untrained individual would be as helpless as a newborn babe were he to be faced with the extraordinarily changed conditions which would confront him at every turn if he were suddenly cast into these other worlds.

Esoteric training is the result of almost innumerable ages of the most careful study by the greatest sages and noblest intellects that the human race has produced. It is no arbitrary study of rules which the student is supposed to follow, although indeed he *is* both supposed and expected to follow certain rules; but it is likewise the making over — or conversion in the original sense of this Latin word — of the personal into the spiritual, and the casting aside of all limitations belonging to ordinary life, for the faculties and powers and the wider fields of action which belong to the initiate or adept in accordance with his degree of growth.

There is nothing so deceptive as the false lights of māyā. Often fine-looking flowers contain deadly poison, either in bud or in thorn; the honey thereof brings death to the soul. No chela is ever permitted to cultivate any psychical powers at any time, until the great foundation has been laid in the evocation of the spiritual and intellectual energies and faculties: vision, will power, utter self-control, and a heart filled with love for all. Such is the law. Therefore not only is it forbidden for the beginner to win and use powers now latent, and to awaken faculties not yet in function within him, but those who may through past karma happen to be born with such awakening inner faculties have to abandon their use when starting their training. And this for the reason that such training is all-round, i.e. every part of the nature must be brought into harmonious and symmetrical relation with every other part before one can tread the path safely.

There comes a time, however, when a pupil is taken individually in hand and instructed how to free the soul so that the body cripples it less, how to become nobler in every way, and this by certain rules of practice and of conduct and thought. First: philosophy, knowing something about the life in the universe; second, discipline; and third, the Mysteries. There is the order; to a certain extent they run concurrently, although each is emphasized in especial when its period arrives.

ESOTERIC DISCIPLINE

To elaborate: the first, philosophy, comprises teaching, with a certain amount of discipline, and an intuition, an intimation, given as to what the Mysteries are. Next, the discipline, with which likewise there are teachings, but, above everything, the neophyte is taught how to control himself, how to be and to do, with a larger intimation of the Mysteries to come. Then, third, the Mysteries, what is called practical occultism, when the individual is worked upon and taught how to release the spirit within him and also his faculties, the while experiencing a still loftier discipline and a loftier philosophy.

Seven are the degrees of initiation. The first three are schools of discipline and learning. The fourth is similar, but greater by far, for in it begins the nobler cycle of initiatory training. It depends upon the individual alone what progress he will make. The disciple is a free man, with free will, and it is his destiny to become a god taking a self-conscious part in the government of the universe. He must therefore choose his own pathway, but beware lest, in exercising the divine faculty of free will his egoism, his selfish propensities, if he have any left, run away with him into the left-hand path. Danger lurks at every step, a danger which is not outside, but in himself.°

Hence discipline is essential all along the line, differing from that which prevails in all stages of human relationships only in this, that it is the origin of those spiritual and ethical principles which have guided the civilizations of the past and the peoples who built them. The basis of this discipline is self-forgetfulness, which is the same as impersonality; and in order to achieve this, other minor rules have been introduced by

---

°It is often asked what guarantee can be proffered by an aspirant against the teachings being wrongfully and perhaps indiscriminately given out by him. There is no absolute guarantee. This is one reason the lines are always so tightly drawn, and why the knock given must be the right knock.

One of the protections against betrayal of the teachings of the higher degrees is the fact that the world would not understand them, and would think the man thus betraying the most sacred truth on earth is a lunatic. People always consider the things which they do not understand as foolishness — how many geniuses in the beginning of their careers have not been thought at least partly mad!

Another protection is that every individual belonging to one of the higher degrees knows perfectly well that a single betrayal means the cessation for him of all teaching for the future, and that every new degree explains the teachings given in the previous one. Consequently a betrayal in the third degree, for example, would mean betraying a 'veil' which itself has to be explained or gone behind in the fourth degree, and so forth through all further degrees.

the sages and seers who were the founders of the mystical schools of former eras.

The rules are simple in themselves, so simple that the novice, unversed in the occult code, is often disappointed at not finding something more difficult to achieve, forgetting that the grandest truths are always the simplest. One such rule is never to strike back, never to retaliate; better to suffer injustice in silence. Another is never to justify oneself, to have patience, and leave the karma to the higher law to adjust. And still another, and perhaps the greatest rule of this discipline, is to learn to forgive and to love. Then all else will come naturally, stealing into the consciousness silently, and one will know the rules intuitively, will be long suffering in patience, compassionate, and great of heart.

Can't we see the beauty of no retaliation, no attempt at self-justification, of forgiveness of injuries, of silence? One cannot take these rules too much to heart; but even so they should be followed impersonally in order that there be no possibility of brooding over real or imaginary hurts. Any rankling sense of injustice would be fatal and would in itself be a doing the very thing, in a passive way, that should be avoided — either passively or actively.

The reason for the prohibition of any effort at self-defense in cases of attack or accusation is training: training in self-control, training in love. For there is no discipline so effective as self-initiated effort. Moreover, the attitude of defense not only hardens the periphery of the auric egg, but also coarsens it throughout; it emphasizes the lower personal self every time, which is a training in the inverse direction, tending toward disintegration, unrest and hatred. Let the karmic law pursue its course. One exercises judgment and discrimination of an exceedingly high type when the consciousness of the effectiveness of this practice is gained. The more a man feels that he, in the light of his conscience, has acted well, the sense of injury, the wish to retaliate, the feverish need of self-justification, become small and unnecessary. Consciousness of right brings forgiveness, and the desire to live in compassion and understanding.

But let us not confuse the rule regarding self-justification with those responsibilities that as honest men and women we may be called upon to fulfill. It may be a clear duty actively to stand up for a principle that is at stake, or to spring to the side of one unjustly attacked. There is a kindness in being rigidly firm, in refusing to participate in evil doing. The sentimental crime of allowing evil to take place before our eyes, and thus participating in it for fear of hurting someone's feelings, is a moral weakness which leads to spiritual degradation. However, when we ourselves are attacked, preferable it is to suffer in silence. Only rarely do we need to justify our own acts.

Overcoming the eager itch of the lower part to prove that 'we are right' may seem a negative exercise, but we shall find that it requires very positive inner action. It is a definite spiritual and intellectual exercise that teaches self-control and brings equanimity. By practicing it, little by little, instinctively one begins to see the viewpoint of the other. Yet here again, there is a subtle danger, for this very practice may become so attractive after one has followed it faithfully for some time, that there is an actual risk of generating and cultivating a spiritual pride in the success thus far achieved. This is something that one must watch for and wrench out of one's soul.

I have known men who struggled and fought so hard to be good that they left a trail of broken hearts behind them, shattered hopes of other human souls — misery brought to others by their frenzied desire to be good. They wanted to advance so greatly that they forgot to be human. Is it wrong to read a good book, to take healthful exercise, or enjoy the food that we eat? Of course not. But if one is strongly attached to something which gives extraordinary pleasure and a duty is neglected, then one should conquer that attachment, for it is doing harm; it is no longer an innocent pleasure, but has become a vice. The simple answer is to forget ourselves and do what we can to benefit others, and we shall be happy, spiritually and intellectually natural and strong, and be respected; and, above everything else, we shall respect ourselves.

This leads on to another thought: it is rare that we make our worst mistakes through our vices; and the reason is that once vices are recognized as such we are seldom swayed by them, but become disgusted and cast them off. In fact, our most serious errors both of feeling and of judgment usually arise out of our virtues — a paradox, the psychological force of which grows upon us as we ponder it.

This can be illustrated by looking at the history of medieval Europe. I believe it is erroneous to suppose that the fanatic monks or ecclesiastical governors who incited those shocking religious persecutions were human devils deliberately excogitating ways of torturing the minds and bodies of their unfortunate fellow men who fell into their power. What they did was diabolic, sheer unconscious devilry, but it arose in their virtues which, because they were so grossly abused, became despicable vices. The most cruel persons usually are not they who are indifferent, but they who are driven by a mistaken ideal, behind which there is a misused moral force. Their virtues, now become unrecognized vices, make them seem for the time completely heartless.

Great thinkers like Lao-tse have pointed out to the confusion of the unthinking that the aggressively virtuous man is the vicious man — an extravagant paradox, and yet one which contains a profound statement of psychological fact. The really dangerous man is not the evil man, for he offends by his intellectual and moral deformity. It is beauty misunderstood and misused that seduces — not physical beauty alone, but beauty in a virtue which has become distorted and misapplied. Virtue itself raises us to the gods; and yet it is our virtues when selfishly applied which so often bring us to do our worst deeds.

There is a deep esoteric meaning in the old injunction: "love all things, both great and small." Hate is constrictive; it builds veils around the individual, whereas love rends those veils, dissolving them and giving us freedom, insight and compassion. It is like the cosmic harmony which manifests in the Music of the Spheres as the stars and planets sing in their courses. Love, impersonal love, harmonizes us with the universe, and this becoming at one with the universe is the last and greatest objective of all phases of the initiatory cycle.

Personal love, on the other hand, is uncharitable and often unlovely, for it is concentrated on one object; it thinks of self rather than of the other; whereas impersonal love gives itself fully, is the very soul of self-sacrifice. Personal love is self-remembrance; impersonal love is self-forgetfulness — there is the distinguishing test. Sentimentality has nothing to do with it; in fact, it is a detriment, for it is an accentuation of the personality. The emotion of love is not love; that belongs to the psychomental and animal side of our being. When we place no frontiers or limits to the current flowing forth from our heart, when we make no conditions as to whether we shall extend our protecting and helpful hand, we shall be as the sun, shedding light and warmth on all. And when love is wholly selfless, it is spiritually clairvoyant, for its vision penetrates to the very essence of the universe.

Among other good and simple rules is to *think* impersonally all the time; in our daily acts to try to detach our interest from them so far as any benefit to our own person is concerned. If we can do them as a work of love, whatever they are, we shall be impersonal naturally, for we shall have lost our self-absorption in the service of others. This is the royal road to self-knowledge, for we cannot become the self universal as long as our attention and thought are concentrated on the limited point of egoity.

Another splendid rule is one that the Lord Buddha gave as a favorite teaching of his to his disciples:

> When evil and unworthy thoughts arise in the mind, images of lust, hatred, and infatuation, the disciple must win from these thoughts other and worthy images. When he thus induces other and worthy images in his mind, the unworthy thoughts, the images of lust, hatred, and infatuation cease; and because he has overcome them his inner heart is made firm, tranquil, unified, and strong.°

All of which means that when we are bothered, tormented perhaps, with selfish and personal impulses and thoughts, we should immediately think of their opposites, holding them steadily in our mind's eye. If we have a thought of hate, we should conjure up a picture of affection and kindness; if of evil-doing, vision a magnanimous and splendid act; if a selfish thought, then imagine ourselves as doing some deed of benevolence, and at all times doing this impersonally. I am inclined to view this as the very best rule of all. It is a fascinating study outside of the benefit that comes: the strengthening of the will, the clearing of vision, the refining of the emotions, the stimulating of the heart-forces and the general growth in strength and nobility of character.

Nevertheless, when a thought has once left the mind, it is impossible to withdraw the energy with which we have charged it; for then it is already an elemental being, beginning its upward journey.† Still, if 'neutralizing' thoughts of an opposite character are immediately sent forth — thoughts of beauty, of compassion, of forgiveness, of a desire to help, of aspiration — the two then coalesce, and the effects of the evil ones are made 'harmless' in the sense that H.P.B. speaks of in *The Voice of the Silence* (p. 55).

°*Majjhima Nikāya,* I, 288.

†Do we realize that every human being is the thought of his own inner god — an imperfect reflection of that inner splendor, nevertheless a child of the thoughts of the divinity within — even as the thoughts of evolving human beings are living entities, embryo-souls developing and moving forward on the pathway of evolutionary growth?

However, I repeat: *a thought can never be recalled.* It is like an action, which once done, is done forever, but is not forever done with. By thinking a noble thought or doing a good deed, following upon an evil impulse, although we cannot recall the evil thought or action and undo it, we can, to a certain extent, render at least less harmful the evil that our wrong thought or act brought about.

We humans are personal precisely in proportion as the spiritual individuality is frittered away in the rays of the lower part of our constitution. When we lose personality, we release the hold which these unprogressed elements have upon our real being. This means a gathering together of the rays hitherto dissipated into the various atomic entities of our lower principles — gathering them into the sheaf of selfhood and thus rebecoming our essential Self. "He that findeth his life shall lose it: and he that loseth his life for my sake shall find it" *(Matthew,* x, 39).

If we can try at every moment to be selfless, we shall forget our personal wants. Our needs it is a duty to attend to, but these usually are not crippling to the spirit. As we strive to become impersonal, we shall in time enter into the universal consciousness — in these few sentences we have the secret and essence of esoteric training. But let us not kill our personality; instead let us use it, thereby changing the direction of its evolutionary tendencies so that the currents of its vitality may flow into the higher consciousness of our individuality. It is a marvelous thought that just to the degree that our individuality increases and our personality decreases, do we rise on the ladder of life towards a more intimate individual union with the cosmic divinity at the center of our solar system. This applies to the vast multitude of the human host, as well as to any other entity of equivalent evolutionary advancement possessing self-consciousness and the other attributes that make man man.

Impersonality, altruism and selflessness: these are magical in their effect upon our fellow men. When we can learn truly to forgive, and to love, the longing of our soul will be self-forgetful service for mankind. No one is too humble to practice it, and no one is so exalted that he can ignore it. The more exalted the position, the more imperative is the call to duty. Singlehanded we may have the world to battle; but even though we go down again and again, we can stand up and remember that the forces of the universe are back of us and on our side. The very heart of Being is with us and we shall win, ultimately, for nothing can withstand the subtle and all-penetrating fire of impersonal love.

In man lies the pathway to wisdom: one who knows himself, whose spiritual nature is brought forth in fuller degree, can comprehend the movements of the planets. One whose inner self is yet more evolved can confabulate with the beings who rule and guide our solar system; one whose entire being is still more unfolded can penetrate into some at least of the arcana of the macrocosm; and so on indefinitely. The higher the development, the larger the vision and the deeper the understanding. The pathway to the universal Self is the path that each individual must himself tread if he wishes to grow, to evolve. No one else can grow for us, and we can grow only along the lines that nature has laid down — the structure of our own being.

Man is indeed a mystery: under the surface and behind the veil there is the mystery of selfhood, of individuality, a career stretching into distant eternities. Man essentially is a godlike energy enshrouded by veils.

MEDITATION AND YOGA

It is in the silence that the soul grows strong. For then it is thrown back upon its own energies and powers, and learns to know itself. One of the finest ways of getting light on a problem quickly and certainly, of cultivating intuition, is by not passing the trouble of solving it on to someone who you believe can help you. Seeing solutions and solving problems are a matter of training, of inner growth. One of the first rules that a neophyte is taught is never to ask a question until he has tried earnestly and repeatedly to answer it. Because the attempt to do so is an appeal to the intuition. It is also an exercise. It strengthens one's inner powers. Asking questions before we have ourselves tried to resolve them simply shows that we are leaning, and this is not good. To exercise our own faculties means growth, the gaining of strength and ability.

Certain questions, however, come with a force that compels an answer. They are like the mystic knocking on the door of the temple; they demand the giving of more light, for they come not from the brain-mind, but from the soul striving to understand the light flowing into it from the perennial fountains of divinity. Ask and ye shall receive; knock — and knock aright — and it shall be opened unto you. If the appeal is strong and impersonal enough, the very gods in heaven will respond. If the individual is very much in earnest, the answer will come to him from within, from the only initiator that any neophyte ever has.

Meditation is a positive attitude of mind, a state of consciousness rather than a system or a time period of intensive brain-mind thinking. One should be positive in attitude, but quietly so; positive as the mountain of granite, and as serene and peaceful, avoiding the disturbing influences of the ever-active and feverish mentality. And, above everything else, impersonal. Meditation in the better sense is the bending of the consciousness, and the raising of the mind to the plane where intuition guides, and where some noble idea or aspiration is native, and the holding of the consciousness in thought there. But one can meditate also on evil things and, alas, many do just this.

It is possible so to meditate before falling asleep that one's soul ascends to the gods, and is refreshed and strengthened by its confabulations with those divine beings. But it is likewise possible to brood before sleep comes so that when the bonds of wakefulness are broken, and the brain-mind is silenced, the soul is dragged downwards, and is thus degraded and weakened. One should never sleep until one has sincerely forgiven all injuries done unto him. This is very important not only as an ennobling practice, but as a much needed protection. Fill the heart with thoughts of love and compassion for all, and the mind with some lofty idea and dwell on it calmly, with the higher, impersonal brooding that is effortless and still, and then there will be a rest of all the senses, and quiet in the mind.

One reason for the need of strict impersonality, without the slightest thought of any destructive or morally offensive element intruding into the heart, such as hate, anger, fear or revenge, or any other of the horrid progeny of the lower self, is that when sleep steals over the body and the ordinary brain-mind consciousness drops away, the soul now released automatically follows the direction last given to it. Thus the practice of calming the mind before retiring can elevate the soul.

Meditate all the time — nothing is so easy and so helpful. Far better is this for most students than to have a set period: quiet, unremitting thought on the questions you have, continuing even when the hands are busy with the tasks of the day, and the mind itself quite absorbed by other duties. In the back of the consciousness there can still be this steady undercurrent of thought. It is likewise a protecting shield in all one's affairs, for it surrounds the body with an aura drawn forth from the deeper recesses of the auric egg, which is ākāśic, and through which, when condensed by the will of one who knows how to do it, nothing material can pass.

Yet even in the profoundest meditation, when one has lost all sense of surrounding circumstances, the trained chela is never in the condition of having lost his spiritual and intellectual grip. He is always alert, always aware that he is in control of the situation, even while the consciousness is passing in review the myriad phases of the subject under contemplation. It is highly inadvisable, as a general rule, to allow oneself to be on another plane in thought so greatly that one becomes a psychic or physical automaton.

There are two kinds of meditation: first, the keeping of some beautiful idea clearly in the mind as a picture, and letting one's consciousness enter into that picture; and second, the casting of the consciousness into higher spheres or planes, and taking in and absorbing the experiences that flow into the consciousness by doing so. But if we set our teeth and grip our hands and mentally hammer this or that point of thought, we are not meditating at all. If we do this, we won't succeed, because such exercise is merely brain-mind cogitation, which is often exhausting, uninspiring and uninspired. There is a difference between just thinking concentratedly on a subject, especially if it means using the brain-mind, and a concentration or absorption of the consciousness in following the ennobling direction along which the spiritual will is guiding.

Meditation, then, is the holding of a thought steady in the mind, and allowing the consciousness to work interiorly upon this thought, easily and with delight. Let it dwell there; let the spirit brood over it. There is no need to put the physical or psychical will on to it. This is true meditation and is really the fundamental secret of yoga, meaning 'union' of the mind with the ineffable peace, wisdom and love of the god within. If one practices this simple rule of jñāna-yoga, after a while it will become natural, a part of the daily consciousness. Concentration or one-pointedness of mind is merely taking this thought into our consciousness more clearly, and centering all our attention upon it — not with the will, but with ease.

All other forms of yoga which depend more or less upon exterior aids, such as posturings, breathings, positions of hands and fingers and feet, etc., belong to the lower parts of hatha-yoga and are little more than crutches, because distracting the mind to these exterior methods and away from the main objective of true yoga itself, which is a reversal of the mind from exterior to inner and spiritual things. Thus all forms of the lower yoga, now become so popular in the West through the 'teachings' of itinerant and wandering 'yogis,' usually do more harm than good.

The hatha-yoga system is a fivefold method of attaining control of the lower psychic faculties through various forms of ascetic practices, requiring a scientific paralyzing of the physical and psychic parts by violent methods. The yogi effects this complete self-absorption by suspending his vital processes and causing a short-circuiting of certain prānic energies of his astro-physical body. As should be obvious, this practice is mentally and physically perilous as well as spiritually restricting, and hence is unequivocally discouraged by all genuinely occult schools. Certain powers can indeed be acquired by these means, but, I repeat, they are powers of the lowest kind, and have no lasting benefit, and, moreover, will greatly hinder one's spiritual progress.

In this connection, William Q. Judge wrote:[*]

> . . . progress will be made. Not by trying to cultivate psychic powers that at best can be but dimly realized, nor by submitting to any control by another, but by educating and strengthening the soul. If all the virtues are not tried for, if the mind is not well based in philosophy, if the spiritual needs are not recognized as quite apart from the realm of psychism, there will be but a temporary dissipation in the astral realms, ending at last in disappointment as sure as the shining of the sun.

On the other hand, the rāja-yoga and jñāna-yoga systems, embracing spiritual and intellectual discipline combined with love for all beings, have to do with the higher portions of the inner constitution — the control of the physical and psychic following as a natural consequence of an understanding of the entire sevenfold man. True yoga controls and raises the mind, thus effecting the communion of the human with the spiritual consciousness, which is relative universal consciousness. The attaining of this union or at-oneness with one's divine-spiritual essence brings illumination.

In certain very exceptional circumstances where a chela has advanced relatively far, mentally and spiritually speaking, but has still a very unfortunate and heavy physical karma not yet worked out, it is proper to use the hatha-yoga methods to a limited degree, but only under the master's own eye. I may add that the *Yoga Aphorisms* (or *Sūtras*) of Patañjali is a hatha-yoga scripture, but one of the highest type. The terse instructions contained in this small work are well known to Western students, largely through the interpretation of W. Q. Judge and later writers.

Real yoga is meditation, as said, and this obviously includes the centering and holding of the mind with fixity on a point of noble thought, and a brooding upon it, pondering upon it. Patañjali in his *Sūtras* (i, 2) wrote: *Yogaś chitta-vritti-nirodhah* — "yoga is the preventing of the whirlings of thought." This is very clear: when the ever-active brain-mind, with its butterfly-like wandering from thought to thought, and its fevered emotions, can be controlled into one-pointed aspiration and intellectual vision upwards, then these 'whirlings' of thinking vanish, and the aspiring organ of thought becomes intensely active, manifests intuition, sees truth,

---

[*] "Answers to Correspondence," December 1893.

and in fact makes the man whose organ of self-conscious thought is so occupied, an imbodiment of wisdom and love — and this is the true yoga. It is the manas, the mind-principle, which is thus active and is, so to speak, turned upon itself upwards instead of downwards, becoming the buddhi-manas instead of the kāma-manas. The *chitta* of the Sanskrit phrase, i.e. the 'thinking,' becomes filled with wisdom and intuition, and the man becomes virtually, when expert in this sublime spiritual exercise, one with the divinity within.

In the next śloka Patañjali goes on to state: "then the Seer abides in himself," the meaning being that the man then becomes a seer, and abides in his spiritual self, the god within him.

Contrariwise, when the mind is not so restrained and directed upwards, then the "whirlings (activity) become assimilated mutually," as the 4th śloka has it — a very concise statement meaning that when the mind is fastened in lower things, its feverish activities enchain the higher manas, which thus becomes temporarily 'assimilated' with its lowest elements, and the man is in consequence no more than the ordinary human being.

An occult secret in connection with the mind is that it takes the form of the object contemplated or perceived, and so molds itself into the objects of thought, whatever their quality. If the mental picture is divine, the mind becomes similar to it because it flows into the divine and molds itself accordingly; and likewise, when the mind is held in the lower things it becomes assimilated to them, because flowing into their form and appearance.°

It is precisely the desire to know, not for oneself, not even for the mere sake of knowing in an abstract sense, but for the purpose of laying knowledge on the altar of service, which leads to esoteric advancement. It is this desire, this will for impersonal service, which purifies the heart, clarifies the mind and impersonalizes the knots of the lower selfhood, so that they open and thereby become capable of receiving wisdom. It is this desire which is the impelling force, the driving engine, carrying the aspirant forward, ever higher and higher.

°This great fact of occultism has therefore a high as well as a low aspect; and this faculty of the mind it is which is used by the adept of either the white or the black class in order to produce, when required, magical effects. Indeed, it is not too much to say that the powers of āveśa, the entering into and using the body of another, as well as the Hpho-wa, or the power of projecting the will and intelligence to other parts, sometimes to incredible distances, depend largely upon this attribute or characteristic of the fluid mind.

THE PĀRAMITĀS AND THE EXALTED EIGHTFOLD PATH

IN BUDDHIST as well as in modern theosophical literature a great deal has been written about the 'glorious virtues' or pāramitās, but unfortunately they have been too often looked upon as being merely a noble but relatively unattainable code of conduct, which indeed they are; but they are more than this. They are actually the rules of thought and action which the would-be chela *must* follow, in the beginning as best he can, but later in completeness, so that his entire life becomes governed and enlightened by them. It is only thus that the disciple can reach what the Lord Buddha called the 'other shore'° — the spiritual realms which have to be reached by crossing the stormy ocean of human existence, and doing so under one's own spiritual and intellectual and psychical power, with only such help as can be given him in view of his own past karma.

The idea of going to the other shore is commonly supposed to be typically Oriental, but this seems unjustified, as many Christian hymns speak of the mystical Jordan and of reaching the 'shore beyond,' a conception which appears to be more or less identic with that of Buddhism. 'This side' is the life of the world, the usual or common pursuits of men. The 'other shore' is simply the life spiritual, involving the expansion in relatively full power and function of the entire range of man's nature. In other words, to reach the 'other shore' means living at one with the

---

°Pāramita and pāragata (or its equivalent pāragāmin) are Sanskrit compounds denoting 'one who has reached the other shore'; pāramitā (the feminine form) is used for the transcendental virtues or attributes which one must cultivate in order to reach that shore. There is a shade of difference in meaning to be noted here: pāramita carries the idea of having 'crossed over' and therefore 'arrived,' while pāragata (or pāragāmin) implies 'departure' from this end and thus 'gone' in order safely to reach the other shore.

Another word of frequent use in Buddhist writings which also imbodies both subtle distinctions of the above term is Tathāgata, a title given to Gautama Buddha. This is a Sanskrit compound that can be divided in two fashions: *tathā-gata*, 'thus gone,' that is, departed for and reached the other shore; and *tathā-āgata*, 'thus arrived or come,' the significance of the term Tathāgata being one who has both 'departed' for and 'arrived' at the other shore, as his predecessor-Buddhas have done.

divinity within, and hence partaking of the universal life in relatively full self-consciousness. The teaching of all the great religious and philosophical systems has been to urge upon their followers the fact that our real goal is to learn the lessons of manifested existence and to graduate from this experience into the cosmic life.

As the *Dhammapada* (verse 85) has it:

There are few people who reach the other shore;
The others run wild on this shore.

A short Buddhist writing called the *Prajñā-Pāramitā-Hridaya Sūtra* or "The Heart or Essence of the Wisdom of the Passing-Over," closes with a beautiful mantra which runs as follows in the original Sanskrit:

Gate, gate, pāragate, pārasamgate, bodhi, svāhā!

O Wisdom! Gone, gone, gone to the other shore,
landed on the other shore, Hail!

Wisdom in this context may be taken as referring to the cosmic buddhi, otherwise called Ādi-buddhi or 'primeval wisdom,' and also in an individualized sense to the supreme Silent Watcher of our planetary chain, Ādi-buddha. The one addressed is he who has arrived at the other shore, the triumphant pilgrim who has become self-consciously at one with the god within him and thus has successfully perceived through the māyā or illusions of the phenomenal worlds. The highest ones who have attained this are jīvanmuktas, 'freed monads'; those less high belong to the different grades in the several hierarchies of the Hierarchy of Compassion.

The discipline of the pāramitās as H.P.B. gave them in *The Voice of the Silence* (pp. 47–8) is as follows:

Dāna, the key of charity and love immortal.

Śīla, the key of Harmony in word and act, the key that counterbalances the cause and the effect, and leaves no further room for Karmic action.

Kshānti, patience sweet, that nought can ruffle.

Virāga, indifference to pleasure and to pain, illusion conquered, truth alone perceived.

Vīrya, the dauntless energy that fights its way to the supernal TRUTH, out of the mire of lies terrestrial.

Dhyāna, whose golden gate once opened leads the Narjol [Naljor] toward the realm of Sat eternal and its ceaseless contemplation.

Prajñā, the key to which makes of a man a god, creating him a Bodhisattva, son of the Dhyānis.

THE PĀRAMITĀS AND THE EXALTED EIGHTFOLD PATH

The manner in which these pāramitās are to be practiced is well illustrated by the following extract from the *Mahāyāna Śrāddhotpāda Śāstra*° which, however, mentions only six, although they are given elsewhere as seven and, when more fully enumerated, as ten:

How should one practise charity (*Dāna*)?

If someone comes and asks for anything, disciples, as far as they are able, should grant the request ungrudgingly and in a way to benefit them. If disciples see anyone in danger, they should try every means they have to rescue him and impart to him a feeling of safety. If any one comes to disciples desiring instruction in the Dharma, they should as far as they are able and according to their best judgment, try to enlighten him. And when they are doing these acts of charity, they should not cherish any desire for recompense, or gratitude, or merit or advantage, nor any worldly reward. They should seek to concentrate the mind on those universal benefits and blessings that are for all alike and, by so doing, will realise within themselves highest perfect Wisdom.

How should one practise virtuous precepts (*Śīla*)?

Lay disciples, having families, should abstain from killing, stealing, adultery, lying, duplicity, slander, frivolous talk, covetousness, malice, currying favor, and false doctrines. Unmarried disciples should, in order to avoid hindrances, retire from the turmoil of worldly life and, abiding in solitude, should practise those ways which lead to quietness and moderation and contentment.... They should endeavor by their conduct to avoid all disapproval and blame, and by their example incite others to forsake evil and practise the good.

How should one practise patient forbearance (*Kshānti*)?

As one meets with the ills of life he should not shun them nor feel aggrieved. Patiently bearing evils inflicted by others, he should cherish no resentment. He should neither be elated because of prosperity, praise, or agreeable circumstances; nor depressed because of poverty, insult, or hardship. Keeping his mind

---

°Often translated as "The Awakening of Faith in the Mahāyāna," but this very inadequately conveys the significance of the original Sanskrit. *Śrāddha* means certainty or confidence based on an unfoldment of inner experiences, the proof of which lies both within and without the self, and implying here a continued process of inner unfoldment, a connotation which is utterly lacking in the word 'faith.' As to *utpāda*, this carries the same idea of continuance and progressive unfoldment, an awakening or rising towards an awareness or realization of wisdom, culminating in the mystic renunciation of the fruits of emancipation and the attainment of buddhahood. This scripture belongs to the *Prajñā-Pāramitā* family of writings, and is usually credited to Aśvaghosha, a notable Buddhist scholar who lived during the latter half of the first century A.D., and whose outstanding work is the *Mahālamkara* or "Book of Great Glory."

concentrated on the deep significance of the Dharma, he should under all circumstances maintain a quiet and equitable mind.

How should one practise courageous vigor (*Vīrya*)?

In the practice of good deeds one should never become indolent. He should look upon any mental or physical suffering as the natural following of unworthy deeds done in previous incarnations, and should firmly resolve that henceforth he would only do those things which are in keeping with a spiritual life. Cherishing compassion for all beings, he should never let the thought of indolence arise, but should ever be indefatigably zealous to benefit all beings. . . .

How should one practise meditation (*Dhyāna*)?

Intellectual insight is gained by truthfully understanding that all things follow the law of causation, but in themselves are transitory and empty of any self-substance. There are two aspects of *Dhyāna:* the first aspect is an effort to suppress idle thinking; the second, is a mental concentration in an effort to realise this emptiness (*śūnyatā*) of Mind-essence. At first a beginner will have to practise these separately but as he gains mind control the two will merge into one. . . .

He should contemplate the fact, that although all things are transitory and empty yet, nevertheless, on the physical plane they have a relative value to those who are cherishing false imagination; to these ignorant ones, suffering is very real — it always has been and it always will be — immeasurable and innumerable sufferings. . . .

Because of all this, there is awakened in the mind of every earnest disciple a deep compassion for the suffering of all beings that prompts him to dauntless, earnest zeal and the making of great vows. He resolves to give all he has and all he is to the emancipation of all beings. . . . After these vows, the sincere disciple should at all times and as far as his strength and mind permit, practise those deeds which are beneficial alike to others and to himself. Whether moving, standing, sitting or lying, he should assiduously concentrate his mind on what should be wisely done and wisely left undone. This is the active aspect of *Dhyāna*.

How can one practise Intuitive Wisdom (*Prajñā*)?

When one by the faithful practice of *Dhyāna* attains to *Samādhi*, he has passed beyond discrimination and knowledge, he has realised the perfect oneness of Mind-essence. With this realisation comes an intuitive understanding of the nature of the universe. . . . he now realises the perfect Oneness of Essence, Potentiality, and Activity in Tathāgatahood. . . .

Prajñā-Pāramitā is highest, perfect Wisdom; its fruitage comes unseen, without effort, spontaneously; it merges all seeming differences whether they be evil or good into one perfect Whole. . . .

Therefore let all disciples who aspire after highest, perfect Wisdom, which is *Prajñā-Pāramitā*, assiduously apply themselves to the discipline of the Noble Path for that alone will lead them to perfect realisation of Buddhahood.

THE PĀRAMITĀS AND THE EXALTED EIGHTFOLD PATH

In order to understand and spiritually to *feel* the true nature of prajñā, it is necessary to abandon the 'this side' view, and in spiritual comprehension to go over to the 'other shore' (pāra), or other manner of looking at things. On 'this side' we are involved in a sphere of consciousness of brain-mind analyses and particulars, which becomes a world of attachments and lower-plane distinctions. When we achieve this inner 'reversal,' this shifting of our consciousness upwards to the mystic 'other shore' of being, we then enter more or less successfully into a world of transcendent realities, from which we can view things in their original and spiritual oneness, beyond the māyā of the deceptive veils of multiplicity; penetrate into the essential nature of these realities and cognize them as they truly are.

This condition of inner clarity and of accurate spiritual and intellectual apperception is so different from the familiar operations of our 'this-side' consciousness in our everyday world of transitory appearances, that untrained minds associate it with the conception of emptiness, vacuity. Emptiness (śūnyatā, to use the Buddhist term), in its true metaphysical meaning, however, should not be confounded with 'nothingness,' implying an absolute negation of real being and thus annihilation. Nor is it to be understood through the ratiocinative faculties of the brain-mind, but rather by the direct or immediate perception belonging to the high spiritual-intellectual state called prajñā, which is above the māyāvi distinctions of being and non-being, of particular and universal, of the many and the one.

Indeed, this high state is the intuitive knowledge and penetrating insight of the spirit-mind in man, his buddhi-manas, which is immeasurably more powerful and penetrating than is mere intellection. Such intuitive knowledge and insight lie ever active in the loftiest and most universal recesses of our consciousness. It is through the gradual awakening of the lower man into self-conscious realization of this spiritual-intellectual consciousness — which in its active manifestations is identic with prajñā — that we arise from the lower realms of our consciousness and escape from the bondage of ignorance and nescience (avidyā), and thus become liberated from the various kinds of both inner and outer pain. This release is the attainment of supreme enlightenment and of emancipation (mukti). In brief, prajñā may perhaps best be translated as intuition, signifying that instant illumination or full knowledge which verily is godlike.

In the *Prajñā-Pāramitā* group of Buddhist scriptures, prajñā is regarded as the directing principle of the other pāramitās, pointing to them as being the method of reaching reality. It is compared to the perceiving and understanding eye that surveys with perfect clearness of vision the horizons of life and designates the path to be followed by the aspirant. Without prajñā, the other pāramitās would be devoid of one of their highest elements; it guides their progressive development, somewhat as the earth provides the fields of sustenance for the growth of vegetation.

All beings in the universe possess prajñā, although it is not functioning self-consciously except when the evolving entities in the course of their evolutionary pilgrimage have become at one with it. The animals have prajñā, including bees and ants, as instances, but any self-conscious awareness thereof is lacking, because such self-realization of union with prajñā begins only with man — at least on this earth. In its first feeble workings prajñā in the human being manifests as aspiration towards illumination, love and wisdom; blossoms in the bodhisattva, and is in full bloom in the Buddhas and Christs, which is the state of perfect enlightenment.

The high chela or initiate who has successfully reached the stage where he has *become* the pāramitās, with his consciousness crystal clear and relatively boundless, his whole being attuned to the spiritual soul of humanity, having given up his self to the selfless glory of living for all that is, is technically called a bodhisattva — 'one whose essence (sattva) is of the very nature of wisdom (bodhi).' The motive which prompts the true disciple to realize within himself supreme enlightenment is never personal gain, however exalted and spiritualized, but the urge to benefit the whole world, to raise all beings from the chains of ignorance and pain, to arouse within himself a compassionate heart for all that lives, so that every sentient being may in time attain to perfect emancipation.°

In the *Mahāprajñāpāramitā* the question is asked of Śāriputra whether the bodhisattva should pay respect only to other bodhisattvas, and not "to all beings generally." To which the sage answers that he should in fact "revere them with the same feeling of self-abnegation as he does the Tathāgatas." He then goes on to say:†

The Bodhisattva should thus awaken a great compassionate feeling towards all beings and keep his mind completely free from arrogance and self-conceit, and let him feel in this wise: I will practise all the skillful means in order to

---

°Cf. Fo-Mu *Prajñāpāramitā*, Fas. 14, Chapter "On Wise Men."
†Hsüan-chuang, Fas. 387, Chapter xii, "On Morality."

THE PĀRAMITĀS AND THE EXALTED EIGHTFOLD PATH

make all sentient beings realize that which is the foremost in themselves, i.e., their Buddha-nature (buddhatā). By realizing this they all become Buddhas, . . .

Prajñā in the individual entity, such as a human being, holds pretty much the same position that Ādi-buddhi or mahābuddhi does in the universe. One of the axioms of the esoteric wisdom is that our universe is an entity; hence we can figurate its individual universal mind or consciousness as a vast ocean of self-conscious buddhi-mānasic energy points. From this standpoint, prajñā may be described as the spiritual individual consciousness of every member of the hosts of dhyāni-chohans or cosmic spirits. Thus when one has attained prajñā-awareness, he is in self-conscious communion with the buddhi-mānasic mind of the Wondrous Being of our hierarchy.

From the foregoing it should be clear that there are numerous differences in grandeur of accomplishment as among the members of a hierarchy, for there are differences in grades of attainment between the chela beginning the path and a mahatma, followed by still higher beings having an even larger realization of prajñā on the ladder of achievement that extends steadily upwards until the Wondrous Being is reached. The prajñā is the same in all; the differences among individuals lie in their respective manifestation of it.

There are also differences of another kind, such as that between one who has attained a relative realization of prajñā and who enters nirvana, and another of similar attainment but who renounces nirvana. Here we have an important distinction based on cosmic ethics: the one who has won nirvana yet renounces it in order to turn back and help the world stands far higher ethically than does the one who enters nirvana for his own bliss. Each has reached a sufficiency of at-onement with prajñā to have gained the nirvanic state, but the one who renounces it has achieved a self-conscious realization of prajñā on a higher buddhic plane than the one who won nirvana and enters into it.

The key to this mystery lies in the fact that every one of the seven principles in the human constitution is septenary, and hence buddhi, which is the seat of prajñā, is sevenfold. We thus see that the one entering nirvana has reached what we may define as kāma-buddhi, but has gone no higher in the quality of his realization of prajñā; whereas the other one who renounced nirvana has attained that condition of buddhic prajñā which we may describe as either buddhi-buddhi or manas-buddhi. The buddhas and mahābuddhas are those who hold what we may call the ātmic state of buddhi — and thus feel themselves absolutely and unqualifiedly self-identified with the universe.

The seven pāramitās as given contain the gist of the code of conduct imbodied in the fuller enumeration of ten pāramitās, or the complete ethical decalog of occultism. The three additional pāramitās are: adhishthāna, upekshā, and prabodha or sambuddhi. Of these adhishthāna, meaning 'inflexible courage,' not merely awaits danger or difficulty, but when enlightened by intuition or prajñā 'goes forwards' and 'stands up' to it. Its natural place follows vīrya or 'fortitude.' The next, upekshā or 'discrimination,' searches for and finds the right method of applying the pāramitās, and appropriately comes after dhyāna. Two terms are given for the tenth pāramitā: prabodha, meaning 'awakenment of inner consciousness,' bringing knowledge and foreknowledge, thus opening up glorious visions on the pathway; and sambuddhi, 'complete or perfect illumination or vision' or self-consciousness of one's identity with the spiritual, the culmination or crown of all. Otherwise phrased, it is 'union with buddhi.'

Other 'virtues' are occasionally included by other schools of esoteric or quasi-occult training in the Orient. As examples, satya or truth, and maitra or universal friendliness or benevolence; but when analyzed these are seen to be already imbodied in the ten pāramitās. Also it may be mentioned here that in many parts of the world there are various systems of training, most of them futile, for on careful examination they will be found to be more or less modifications of hatha-yoga, and, as pointed out, these are extremely dangerous even at the best, and at the worst will produce insanity or loss of the soul.

Strength is born from exercise, and it is the exercising of our strength in the tests and experiences of daily life that in time leads to the treading of the path. Unless the student follow the inner discipline, which is the continuous and never-failing practice of the spirit of these ten glorious virtues or pāramitās as his inflexible rule of thought and of action from day to day, he will never succeed in his endeavors. It is just this discipline, this exercising of his will power and of his intelligence and of the love which should fill his heart, which eventually bring the neophyte to the new or 'second' birth, which produce the dvija, the 'twice-born,' the initiate, finally to become the master of life and of death.

THE PĀRAMITĀS AND THE EXALTED EIGHTFOLD PATH

The reader may be wondering just what connection the pāramitās have with the much more familiar teachings of Buddhism, known respectively as the Four Noble Truths and their logical corollary the Eightfold Path. The connection is both historical and intimate, for both contain the same root-ideas, only in the more popular teaching so phrased as to furnish a code of conduct which the average worldly man is capable of following, if he desire to avoid the harassing mistakes attendant upon human life, and to attain the peace and intellectual detachment which accompany a life well and nobly lived.

Briefly, the Four High Truths are: first, that the cause of the suffering and heartache in our lives arises from attachment or 'thirst' — trishnā; second, that this cause can be made to cease; third, that the cessation of the causes productive of human sorrow is brought about by living the life which will free the soul from its attachment to existence; and the fourth truth, leading to the extinction of the causes of suffering, is verily the Exalted Eightfold Path, to wit: "right belief, right resolve, right speech, right behavior, right occupation, right effort, right contemplation, right concentration."

Now this course of endeavor was called by the Buddha the Middle Way, because it involved no useless or fanatical asceticism on the one hand, and no laxity of principle and of thought and consequent behavior on the other hand. It is a code, as said, that is within the reach of every man or woman, calling for no special conditions or circumstances, but able to be practiced by anyone who yearns to better his life, and to do his part in helping to bring about the surcease of the world-misery surrounding us, and of which sensitive human hearts everywhere are conscious.

It must not be supposed, however, that the chela neglects the ethical injunctions of the Eightfold Path, for this would be a misapprehension of their import. In fact, he not only practices them, but does so with far greater concentration of mind and heart than the average man, because at the same time he is striving with all his soul to raise himself to the sublime altitude of the pāramitās by which he should live.

It is perhaps necessary to weigh somewhat strongly upon this point, because there is a totally erroneous idea current among some half-baked mystics that it is a part of the chela's life to ignore normal human relations, to take small account of them, and to imagine that he is freed from his duties, even of a worldly kind, towards his fellow men. This last supposition runs directly counter to all the teaching of occultism.

The principle behind the Four High Truths and their eight corollaries is this: if the root of attachment — desire — can be cut, the soul thereupon becomes freed, and in thus liberating itself from the chains of desire which bring about attachment, the cause of sorrow is made to cease; and the way of cutting the root of attachment is by so living that gradually the thirst of the soul for the things of matter dies. When this happens, the individual is 'free' — he has become a relatively perfected jīvanmukta, a master of life. Once he has reached this stage of utter detachment, he is a bodhisattva, and thereafter devotes himself completely to all beings and things, his heart filled with infinite compassion and his mind illuminated with the light of eternity. Thus it is that as a bodhisattva he appears again and again on earth, either as a buddha or as a bodhisattva, or indeed remains in the invisible worlds as a nirmāṇakāya.

The common idea regarding the bodhisattva, that he has only one more incarnation to undergo before he becomes a buddha, is correct as far as it goes, but as thus expressed is inadequate. As a matter of fact, the ideal both of esoteric theosophy and esoteric Buddhism is the bodhisattva, even more, perhaps, than the buddha, for the reason that the bodhisattva is one whose whole being and objective, whose whole work, is the doing of good unto all beings, and the bringing of them safely to the 'other shore'; whereas the buddha, while the same thing in an extended degree, nevertheless, by the very fact of his buddhahood in the present stage of spiritual unfoldment of the human race, is on the threshold of nirvana, and usually enters therein. It is, of course, quite possible for a buddha to refuse the nirvana and to remain on earth as a bodhisattva or a nirmāṇakāya; and in this last case, as a Buddha of Compassion he is at once a buddha by right and a bodhisattva by choice.

Too much stress cannot be laid upon the great need of understanding the inner significance of the bodhisattva doctrine, imbodying as it does the spirit of occult teaching running throughout the cycle of initiatory training as well as in the nobler schools of the Mahāyāna. It is at once seen why in northern Buddhism the bodhisattva is so greatly honored and occupies so lofty a position in the reverence of human hearts. For the Buddhas of Compassion are such because they themselves imbody this ideal when they renounce the spiritually selfish bliss of nirvanic buddhahood in order to remain in the world to work for it. Even the humblest and least educated can aspire towards this ideal.

In future aeons one must choose whether he will become one of the

THE PĀRAMITĀS AND THE EXALTED EIGHTFOLD PATH

Buddhas of Compassion or one of the Pratyeka-Buddhas. When the choice comes, it will come as the karmic resultant of lives previously lived, for it results from the bent of one's character, the spiritual faculties aroused, the will made to be alert, responsive to command: all these will govern and in fact make the choice when the time for choosing arrives. Therefore the training starts now: becoming great in small things, one learns to become great in great things.

As a final thought, one must not be heavy in living the life which the High Eightfold Path, or indeed the pāramitās, enjoin. He should joy in so doing. For I sincerely believe that everyone who practices these noble rules to some extent at least will be enormously bettered by them. Nor can we be oblivious of how greatly such consistent practice will increase the will power, strengthen the mind, enlarge the sympathies of the heart, and bring about a glorious illumination of soul, all of which in their final stages produce the mahatma — the true bodhisattva.

THE INITIATORY CYCLE

The core of our being is pure consciousness, and in proportion as we ally ourselves with our inner god, with that pure monadic consciousness, shall knowledge come to us naturally. Our understanding will expand, and finally become cosmic, and we shall then realize that there is another cosmos still grander of which our cosmos is but an atom. This is the path of evolution, of growth, inner and outer; it is the pathway of initiation, the pathway to almighty love and compassion.

The word initiation comes from a Latin root meaning to begin, and esoterically it connotes a new becoming, an entering upon a course of life and study which eventually will bring out all of the spiritual and intellectual grandeur that the individual has within him. It is in fact a hastening of the evolutionary process: not in the sense of omitting any stage, but in condensing within a short period what in the natural course would take aeons of striving to attain.

Esoteric training, therefore, is often painful, for it means accelerated growth, doing rapidly and vigorously what in nature's ordinary procedures would take many, many tens of thousands of years, millions perhaps. It is painful at times because, instead of slowly growing to see the beauty and harmony of life everywhere, one must learn to master oneself with an iron will; to forget oneself utterly, to serve all: to give up one's self for the universal self, to die daily so that one can live the cosmic life.

I suppose that every human being takes it for granted that from the time he first issued forth from the bosom of the Infinite as an unself-conscious god-spark until he reattains divinity as a self-conscious god, he will fail, and fail many times, but that ultimately he will achieve — if he rises and presses forwards. The failure is not so much. It is the going backwards, the stopping and allowing the evolutionary current to sweep by, leaving one in the rear: this is morally wrong. It is our duty to go forwards; to become impersonal, self-forgetful. Obviously, the expression 'going backwards' does not imply an actual retrograde motion of a body. The idea is adapted from human experience. We may set out with high courage and leaping ambition to do something, and then discouragement overtakes us and we turn back, leaving the deed undone. Strictly speaking, going backwards is impossible, for nature closes the door behind us at every instant; nor does it mean undoing what evolution has brought to pass. Rather it denotes plunging farther into matter instead of rising more fully into spirit; in other words, changing the direction of our evolutionary journey.

Never was there a mahatma who had not failed and failed many, many times. Failure is unfortunate, but it can be remedied; and by the will of the strong turned into victory. To quote the words of W. Q. Judge:*

> We may "fail" in specific acts or endeavor, but so long as we continue to persevere such are not "failures" but lessons necessary in themselves. Through resistance and effort we acquire fresh strength; we gather to ourselves — and by occult laws — all the strength we have gained by overcoming. Entire "success" is not for us now, but continuous, persistent effort is, and *that* is success and not the mere carrying out of all our plans or attempts. Moreover no matter how high we go in Nature, there are always new rungs of the ladder to mount — that ladder whose rungs are all mounted in labor and in pain, but also in the great joy of conscious strength and will. Even the Adept sees fresh trials before him. Remember also when we say "I have failed" it shows that we have had and still have aspiration. And while this is so, while we have before us loftier heights of perfection to scale, Nature will never desert us. We are mounting, and aspiring, and the sense of failure is the surest proof of this. But Nature has no use for anyone who has reached the limits of, or outlived, his aspirations. So that every "failure *is* a success." At the outset the greater your aspirations the greater the difficulties you will encounter. Forget not then that to continue to try even when one constantly fails is the only way to come to *real* success.

The aim of initiation is to ally the human being with the gods, which is begun by making the neophyte at one with his own inner god. It means not only an alliance with the divinities, but also that the initiant, the learner, if he succeed, will pass behind veil after veil: first of the material universe, and then of the other universes within the physical-material one, each new passing behind a veil being the entering into a grander mystery. Briefly, it is the self-conscious becoming-at-one with the spiritual-divine universe; enlarging the consciousness, so that from being merely human it takes unto itself cosmic reaches. The man in his thought and consciousness thus is at home in every part of universal Being — as much at

---

Answers to Correspondence, September 1892.

home on Sirius or on the Polar Star as he is on Canopus or on earth, and even more so as regards the invisible worlds.

Initiation is a quickening of the process of evolution, an enlivening of the inner man as contrasted with the outer physical person. In its higher stages, it brings with it powers and an unfolding of the consciousness which are verily godlike; but also does it imply the taking over unto oneself of godlike responsibilities. No one becomes an esotericist merely by signing a slip of paper; he cannot become such unless some gleam of buddhic light shines in his heart and illumines his mind. A natural esotericist is one who is born with at least a glimmer of the Christ-light shining within. Such a one sooner or later, as surely as the working of karma pursues its invariable course, is attracted to the path, for it is the working out of his destiny, trained and shaped in the past, into his character as it now is, and in its fruition blossoming forth into an instinctual recognition of truth.°

The least and virtually negligible part of initiation is the ritual. No initiation can be conferred upon another. All growth, all spiritual illumination, takes place *within oneself*. There is no other way. Symbolic rites and outer paraphernalia are but aids to the learner, aids to the developing of the power of the inner vision, the inner eye. Therefore any initiatory trial, no matter where had or what the arrangements may be, is in essence an individual inner opening. Were it not so, there could be no initiation

---

°There are occasional cases of individuals who have been chelas in past lives, but who have stumbled on the path and broken the link in some very unfortunate way for themselves with their teacher. Yet because of past excellencies, when the next or possibly a second incarnation occurs, they come into life endowed with unusual powers or faculties; they enter with a reservoir of garnered inner spiritual, intellectual and psychical experiences which give them light, and help them to keep touch with the god within.

H.P.B. has called these the nurslings of the nirmāṇakāyas, and points to Jacob Boehme as an instance. There was an individual who through some willfulness of a serious character had broken the link, yet had advanced sufficiently far so that he did not lose the spiritual attainments he had made. Although no longer a direct chela, he was nevertheless watched over, aided, and his future progress gently stimulated, so that in the next life (or even at the end of the life he last lived as Jacob Boehme), he may again make or have made the conscious link. In other words, Boehme had spiritual experiences; he initiated himself from the fountain of light within himself, gained in former days when he was an accepted chela. In reality, as said, all initiation is self-initiation, self-awakening. A teacher merely guides, helps, comforts, stimulates and supports. Cf. *The Secret Doctrine*, I, 494.

THE INITIATORY CYCLE

except as a hollow ritual, much as are the sacraments of the churches today for the most part; even so, they are reflections, however faint, of once living experiences of chelas undergoing initiation.

The ancient Mysteries of Greece, for example, those conducted by the State at Eleusis and Samothrace, or at Delphi, or again those which took place at the Oracle of Trophonius, were largely ceremonial. Yet in all of them, even in the degenerate days, there was also a certain amount of actual spiritual experience. I might add that the hints found in literature of the ordeals to be faced and overcome should not be construed too literally; they are not imaginary exactly, but are symbolic representations of what the initiant has to meet in himself. For thoughts are mental entities and therefore have form and power of their own, and the individual must win over his lower nature, or fail.

There are actually ten degrees in the initiatory cycle, but only the seven that pertain to the seven manifested planes of the solar system need concern us — the three highest being utterly beyond present human understanding; and they will remain so until our consciousness will have become virtually universal, ultrahuman. These seven degrees are the seven great portals through which the pilgrim must pass before he attains quasi-divinity. Between each of these portals there are seven smaller doors through which one must pass, each being a step in training, in schooling, so that all in all there are forty-nine stages, just as there are forty-nine planes in our solar system: seven great planes and seven subplanes or minor spheres or kingdoms in each of the primal seven.

The first three grades or degrees are concerned with study, with unceasing aspiration to grow spiritually and intellectually, to evolve and become greater; and also with living the life. These are symbolic, i.e. dramatic in form so far as the rites go. There is likewise teaching (which is the main part of these rites) about recondite secrets of nature, teaching which is rarely given in a reasoned and consecutive form because that is the brain-mind way, but suggested by a hint here, an allusion there. The method is not to fill the mind of the learner full of other men's thoughts, but to arouse the spiritual fire in himself which brings about an awakening of the understanding, so that in very truth the neophyte becomes his own initiator.

What one receives from outside in the way of ideas, of thoughts, are merely the outward stimuli, arousing the inner vibration preparing for the reception of the light within. Transference of ideas is but a method of speaking. Impressions are made, which set up the corresponding vibratory chord in the recipient's psychological apparatus, and instantly the corresponding knowledge flashes from the recipient's own mind above. Devotion to truth, to the point of utterly forgetting oneself, opens the channel of reception. Light and knowledge then enter the mind and heart — from oneself, from one's inner god, which thus is awakened or, more correctly, begins to function, temporarily though it be; and it is in this wise that the man initiates himself. The whole process is based on nature's laws, on the natural growth of understanding, of interior vision.

With the fourth initiation begins a new series of inner unfoldings — that is to say, not only are the study, the aspiration, and the living of the life, continued in the future stages, but with this degree something new occurs. From that moment the initiant starts to lose his personal humanity and to merge into divinity, i.e. there ensues the beginning of the loss of the merely human and the commencing of the entering into the divine state. He is taught how to leave his physical body, how to leave his physical mind, and to advance into the great spaces not alone of the physical universe, but more especially of the invisible realms as well. He then learns to become, to be, to enter into the intimate consciousness of the entities and spheres he contacts.

The reason for this is that in order fully to know anything, one must *be* it; temporarily, at least, one must *become* it, if he would understand precisely what it is in all its reaches. His consciousness must merge with the consciousness of the entity or thing which he is at that instant learning to know the meaning of. Hence the quasi-mystical stories of the 'descent' of the initiant into 'hell' in order to learn what the life of the hellions is, and what their sufferings are; and also partly in order to bring out the compassion of the one experiencing what these entities go through as the karmic result of their own misdeeds. And equally, in the other direction, the initiant must learn how to become at one with the gods and to confer with them. To understand their nature and their life, he must for the time being himself become a god; in other words, enter into his own highest being.

Thus beginning with this fourth initiation the neophyte slips into new realms of consciousness; the spiritual fires of the inner constitution are most potent both in character and in functioning; the spiritual electricity, so to speak, flows with far more powerful current. One cannot really put these mystical things into everyday words. In addition to the teachings and the symbolic or dramatic ritual, the neophyte — and he is always such, no matter how high the degree may be — learns how to control nature's forces and become able to accomplish such wonders as consciously leaving the body, leaving our planet in order to pass to other centers of the solar system.

The fifth degree is along the same pathways of experience, when the man becomes a master of wisdom and compassion. In this degree there comes the final choice: whether, like the great Buddhas of Compassion, one will return to help the world, to live for it and not for self; or whether, like the Pratyeka-Buddhas, one will go forwards on the pathway of self — merely self-development.

The sixth initiation runs to still loftier realms of consciousness and experience; and then comes the last and supreme initiation, the seventh, which comprises the meeting face to face with one's divine self, and the becoming-at-one with it. When this occurs, he needs no other teacher. It also includes individual communication with the supreme Mahāchohan, who is practically identical with what has been called the Silent Watcher of the human race.

Each degree stands on its own basis of rule and training. Nevertheless, the one rule runs through all, to wit, that the supreme guide for the neophyte is the god within himself, which is his final spiritual and intellectual tribunal, and in second order only comes his teacher. To such the disciple gives glad allegiance — but in no case blind obedience — for he knows by this time that his own inner god and the inner god of the teacher are both sparks of Alaya's self.

I might add that the higher the degree, the more informal and less ritualistic become the relations between teacher and pupil, and the more is the pupil expected to strive to live in and to be at one with his inner divine monitor. Further, in the more advanced stages no record of any kind is made. It is solely the memory of the auditors which is trained to receive and to retain what has been impressed upon it, a training which a dependence upon written notes could never bring about. Neither in writing, in paint, in cipher nor in engraving, are the teachings committed to visible record; they are carried in the mind and in the heart alone.

The whole endeavor is to arouse the will power, the individuality, and the native faculties of the inner god. The transmission of intelligence, therefore, passes at low breath and with mouth to ear, to use the old saying. In the highest degrees not even this is permitted, for the neophyte, the recipient of esoteric knowledge and wisdom, has become so trained that he can receive by thought-transference, as it were, and need not even be in the presence of his teacher. More and more the teacher communicates through the soundless sound, the voice of the silence, the voice in which the teachings 'uttered' opens the spiritual vistas within the disciple.

Every step forwards is a going into a greater light, in comparison with which the light just left is shadow. No matter how high one stands on the ladder of evolution, even as high as the gods, there is always one other just ahead, one who knows more than he; and ahead of him there is a constantly ascending range of entities of progressively vaster cosmic consciousness. The hierarchical stream is nature's basic framework; hence, none of us is without a teacher, for there is the infinite universe above us — hierarchies of life and of evolutionary experience far superior to ours.

Consequently, when the monadic essence of a man, after leaving our own hierarchy, advances into the sublimer realms of cosmic Being, he does so as an embryo-entity, therein beginning his next upward climb on the first round of that new ladder of life, when perforce he will need someone to guide his steps. And that need for guides and teachers will remain until, in the course of the cycling ages, he will have climbed higher and higher to the topmost rung of *that* ladder of life, when again he shall become at one with that still sublimer mystery of the inmost of the inmost of his being. And to this sublimer mystery what name can we give? Human language fails, and only the spiritual imagination can soar into the spheres of the divine. Thus the evolving entity passes continually from one to another range of life, from one to another hierarchy of ineffable experience — and thus forwards forever. Is it not self-evident that one is always a learner in the school of life, for there are veils upon veils covering the face of eternal Reality?

When once the spiritual understanding has come, forgetfulness can never thereafter ensue. It is precisely in the inability to wipe out from the memory the glory seen and almost touched that lies the wretchedness of failure undergone by the unsuccessful aspirant. He who has never experienced heaven, yearns toward it, and with hope of success; whereas he who has skirted its boundaries and had a glimpse of the supernal through its portals, and then fails to pass within, will remember enough to fill his soul with agony and even despair at the remembrance of the vision seen and lost.

THE INITIATORY CYCLE

When it comes to the severe tests, terrific as they are in the more advanced degrees, the mentality must be such that it will repel outside influences of the most persuasive character. Such influences arise in impressionability, at once a great virtue, but in many respects a fatal weakness; and another psychological factor to be carefully watched is the too strong and too quick logical faculty of the brain-mind. The mentality must be rigidly subordinated to the nobler attributes and not usurp the place of mastery; if it is made subservient, then it is of genuine value. The higher mind rooted in the buddhi principle has an infallible logic as well as an infallible intuition of its own, of which the brain-mind procedures are pale and usually distorted reflections, and because of this are often most dangerous enemies.

One cannot trifle with occultism with impunity. The entire nature is aroused, and the battle with the lower self at times may take on the character of desperation, for the neophyte instinctively feels that he must conquer or fail. But if he perform faithfully the first duty that comes to hand, no matter how humble and simple, that is his path. In conquering our own weaknesses, we help not only our own nature, but all mankind; more, we help every sentient, living thing, for we are at one with the very forces which are the circulations of the universe.

To achieve the bond of union with one's essential Self is the supreme aim of initiation.° It is the pathway to the gods, which means making of each one of us an individual divinity. The following of this pathway is a most serious, a most sacred undertaking. It will call forth every particle

---

°For some reason there has been a singular misapprehension among a few to the effect that the highest initiations are denied to women. This is not the case. There is nothing in the world that prevents a woman from reaching the noblest pinnacle of attainment, from passing successfully the most severe tests of initiation. However, those who take the highest initiations usually do so in a man's body, simply because it is easier, the psychological and physiological apparatuses being better prepared for passing those initiations. But it is downright foolish to suppose that initiation in any age past or present has been or is the prerogative or especial privilege of men.

One has but to recall the long and uninterrupted line of prophetesses, even in the anthropomorphic and materialistic civilizations of historic Greece and Rome, to realize that women had their place in the temple schools and achieved high and outstanding honors in the esoteric training. The Oracle at Delphi is perhaps the most widely known; other examples are the Celtic Druids and the Germanic peoples who were famous in antiquity for their women leaders, their seeresses and prophetesses. However much women initiates may have kept behind the veil of seclusion, their inner capacity and power to achieve were universally recognized.

of strength, of will power, that one's nature contains, if one wishes to go forward to the sublime ultimate. How to achieve this is by totally ignoring the knot of personality, thus passing into the smooth, orbital movement of consciousness existing around the central core of one's being, and then finally to blend and become at one with the sublime wonder, the divinity within.

Behind every veil there is another, but through them all shines the light of truth, the light that liveth forever within every one of us, for it is our inmost self. Every human being in the core of the core of his essence is a sun, destined to become one of the starry hosts in the spaces of Space, so that even from the very first instant when the divine-spiritual part of us begins its peregrinations throughout universal Being, it is already a sun in embryo, a child of some other sun that then existed in space. Initiation brings forth this inner, latent, stellar energy in the heart of the neophyte.

Aham asmi Parabrahman, I am the boundless All — beyond both space and time. This idea is the very keystone of the temple of ancient truth. It is mother nature in her divine, spiritual, psychological, ethereal, and physical reaches that is our universal home — a home having no specific location because it is everywhere.

Here, then, is the pathway by which any son of man may ascend, if he have the inflexible will to do so and the yearning for a greater light. He may rise along the different stages of the hierarchy, taking each step upwards through an initiation until his being finally becomes at one with the Silent Watcher of our globe. Then, at a period still more distant, his monad will become at one with the Silent Watcher of our planetary chain and, at a period still more remote in cosmic time, he will become identified as an individual monadic life-center with the hierarch of our solar universe.

The inmost of us *is* the inmost of the universe: every essence, every energy, every power, every faculty, that is in the boundless All is in each one of us, active or latent. All the great sages have taught the same verity: "Man, know thyself," which means going inwards in thought and feeling, in ever-greater measure allying ourselves self-consciously with the divinity at the core of our being — the divinity which also is the very heart of the universe. There, indeed, is our home: boundless, frontierless Space.

Appendix

Foreword and Contents
from *Fountain-Source of Occultism*

Foreword

A WORK OF ART stands or falls by its power to inspire. With a book such as FOUNTAIN-SOURCE OF OCCULTISM, which treats of cosmic truths and man's timeless search for answers, all the more must its message stand or fall on worth alone. Of this G. de Purucker is pre-eminently aware; he does not profess to provide the definitive statement, the final word of truth. What he does offer is an illumined interpretation of the universal wisdom on which the Secret Doctrine of the ages — and of H. P. Blavatsky's masterpiece of that name — is founded.

Born on January 15, 1874 in Suffern, Rockland County, New York, de Purucker lived in the United States until the late '80's when the family moved to Geneva, Switzerland. His father, an Episcopal minister, had been appointed chaplain of the American Church there; a learned man and utterly committed, his inmost wish was to have his son ordained in the Anglican Communion. So he personally taught the boy Latin, Greek and Hebrew, had him tutored in modern European languages, as well as in the history and literature of Biblical peoples and of ancient Greece and Rome.

The youth applied himself with assiduity, but his was a profoundly inquiring mind, with a natural intuitive sense of what was spiritually true and what was counterfeit. Before he reached eighteen, he knew with certainty that he could not enter the church; that, in fact, no formal religion could ever bind him. The quest for the gnosis, the living wisdom behind the externals of rite and dogma, had taken powerful hold.

The shock to the parents was grievous: here was their son, destined from childhood for the ministry, able to read the Holy Scriptures in their original tongues, and trained in the functions and responsibilities of a pastor — turned agnostic.

Deeply troubled, the young man left his home and studies in Geneva, sailed for America and, after spending a few months in New York, came to California where he worked on various ranches in San Diego County. All the while he continued his search, "looking around me, right and left, trying to find the clue to the mysteries of life and death which were bothering me so badly." He bought books on the Tarot as well as on mind-healing, to find they did not satisfy. When he came across a translation of one of the Upanishads, he set to work to master Sanskrit, just as he had earlier perfected himself in Anglo-Saxon, believing with Heine, the poet, that "with every new language, one wins a new soul."

Then one day, he tells us, a small book on Theosophy fell into his hands, and "it startled me":

I saw high thinking! I felt that there was more in this book than what an agnostic had seen. My years of study and reading of the literatures of the world — ancient literatures especially — had taught me to recognize ancient truth when I saw it. I was fascinated with something that I had always known in my heart; and it was this, that there has always existed, and that there exists today, a band, a company, a society, an association, of noble Sages, great Seers, "Wise Men of the East," as this book called them.

We do not know the name of the book, but we do know that on August 16, 1893, Hobart Lorenz Gottfried de Purucker (later known as G. de P. to his associates) joined the Theosophical Society then headed in America by William Q. Judge, co-founder in 1875 with H.P. Blavatsky and H.S. Olcott of the modern theosophical movement. As a member of the San Diego Lodge and a regular user of their library, de Purucker helped organize a *Secret Doctrine* Class, and though only nineteen soon was appointed "permanent reader," moderating and guiding the studies of the members, most of whom were considerably older than he. For the next 49 years, to the day of his death on September 27, 1942, G. de P. gave of the fullness of himself in the service of his fellow men — a service which was to find magnificent expression in his elucidation of the spiritual principles of theosophy.

Everything he said, in private or in public print, was an amplification of his youthful vision of the Oneness of the divine impress, and of the experiencibility of that Oneness by every human being. FOUNTAIN-SOURCE OF OCCULTISM is no exception.

In July 1929, when Gottfried de Purucker succeeded Katherine Tingley to the leadership of the Theosophical Society with international headquarters then at Point Loma, California, he initiated a series of esoteric studies for the purpose of stimulating the seeds of altruism as well as of giving instruction in the deeper aspects of theosophy. No question was too simple, none too complex, for careful examination. He insisted,

FOREWORD

however, that always the 'scientific-philosophical' points of doctrine be infused with the 'ethical-mystical': only as one lived the teaching he learned about would it yield its esoteric content.

The present volume derives from twelve booklets of instruction privately printed in 1936. These had been compiled by a small committee under Dr. de Purucker's general supervision from the stenographic reports of esoteric meetings held by him from 1929 to 1933, to which he added certain relevant passages from his published works, as well as a copious amount of fresh material on a wide variety of subjects.

Of particular interest is the order of presentation, as he had himself arranged this with exceeding care. His primary concern, he explained, was to allow the student at the outset — before he might be caught up by the fascination of the highly philosophical teachings later developed — full opportunity to absorb the ideal of unselfish service, which marks the path of compassion chosen by mankind's spiritual Mentors. Moreover, when asked why he had started off the strictly doctrinal portion of the series with an abstruse treatise on Space and Māyā, instead of with the practical themes of karma and rebirth which are easily grasped, he countered that those ideas were already dealt with abundantly in the published literature of the Society. His whole endeavor was to raise the student's consciousness out of the narrow confines of the purely personal into cosmic reaches where even the knottiest of human problems could be seen in truer proportion.

Obviously, then, the book presupposes some knowledge of basic theosophical thought. But does this mean it has little to offer those to whom these ideas may be new? Quite the contrary, for here is food for reflection for all seekers, whatever their spiritual or religious leanings; and equally for those who have broken away from their credal moorings and are seeking a philosophy of meaning to which they can anchor. In brief, it addresses itself to all who recognize the interrelatedness of human destiny to the cosmic design; who intuitively sense that the pilgrimage of man spans a multiplicity of lives on earth so that the soul in the course of ages can bring forth its latent godhood. Above all, it speaks to those who in their most private moments feel the call of the inward way, to find the still, small path and take the ancient vow of self-dedication to the service of mankind.

There may be some, perhaps, who might wish that Dr. de Purucker had limited his use of foreign terms to the minimum, and presented the theosophical viewpoint simply, with a clear-cut exposition of theme. For in FOUNTAIN-SOURCE, in tracing the descent of spirit into matter and its reascent to its pristine source, we read of lokas and talas, of planes and dhātus, of monads and sheaths.

There is sound reason for the use of so rich a terminology, drawn from the religious and philosophic treasuries of Orient and Occident. The root ideas are identic, but each lightbringer transmits his vision of Reality through the lens of his own initiatory experience. Consequently, every spiritual seer gives what appears to be a unique presentation, when actually he is simply clothing in different outer form the same occult verity. It was not only to enrich the understanding of those attached to a particular faith, but likewise to aid students of comparative religion, philosophy and mythology that Dr. de Purucker exhaustively demonstrates that the many and various names in the ancient literatures for God and the gods and their manifold functions are but variant manners of describing the *one* evolutionary process.

But the book is more than an orderly treatment of doctrine; rather is it a quickener of the intuition. If the reader can follow the author's sometimes tenuous yet always unbreakable sequence of thought, he may discover, in a sudden flash of insight, what H.P.B. was actually saying in this or that "difficult" passage. What was formerly baffling even to the very astute, may become, often without his brain-mind being aware of it, luminous with practical wisdom.

However, just because the volume before us consistently delineates this and that teaching in *The Secret Doctrine* or *The Mahatma Letters*, let it not be thought that the author regards the writings of H.P.B. or her teachers as "a final test of infallible authority, the way the Christians have set up their Bible and then worshiped it" — to quote from a letter G. de P. wrote on June 14, 1932 to A. Trevor Barker. "If that were the case, we would never evolve. H.P.B.'s books would be sacrosanct. . . . We must stand for the principles of things. It is very important."

Time and again the author reminds us that the only authority, the only real initiator, for each individual is his own higher self. The paradox is that Dr. de Purucker does speak "as one with authority," the authority of profound spiritual experience. Because of this many, many doors are opened wide, although as many remain closed or only slightly ajar, awaiting the moment when the reader himself will give the knock that will open for him the doorway to the light of his own inner god. To place reliance solely on head learning, the eye doctrine, is to gain but little of permanent worth. It is the heart doctrine that should claim our allegiance, the heart wisdom that makes the impress on the soul.

Significantly, G. de Purucker, as early as 1935, publicly expressed the hope, if he could find "the time and strength so to do, to publish another volume or two containing Theosophical teaching" which up to then had been privately circulated. What had formerly been held as esoteric, he believed would even then be understood in greater measure, due to the "more awakened intelligence of modern men," as well as to the increased "receptivity to new ideas [which] has created an entirely different and indeed fallow field of consciousness" (*The Esoteric Tradition*, p. x). While he himself was unable to accomplish this, one of these projected works, *The Dialogues of G. de Purucker,* representing the meetings of the Katherine Tingley Memorial Group, was issued in 1948 by Arthur L. Conger. Now with the publication of FOUNTAIN-SOURCE OF OCCULTISM, both of these hoped-for volumes of hitherto esoteric material are available for students everywhere.

It is our deep regret that James A. Long, leader of the Theosophical Society from 1951 to 1971, did not live to see this work in finished form. But the guidelines he laid down in 1966 for the editing and preparation of the manuscript have been faithfully followed: to preserve the integrity of the teaching, both in atmosphere and content; to eliminate unnecessary repetitions; delete any purely organizational matters relating to the Theosophical Society or Esoteric Section; anglicize the spelling of those Sanskrit and other foreign terms now in current usage, such as karma, mahatma, etc.; and, where advisable, lift the presentation out of its private esoteric setting into a form suitable to public print. In brief, to condense and distill from the twelve booklets the marvelous treasury of wisdom contained therein so that the world may benefit.

As Mr. Long conceived Dr. de Purucker's intent:

All of this doctrinal esotericism is for one purpose, and one purpose only — not merely to satisfy the intellect of the reader, but to lay the groundwork for the development of the compassionate side of our nature in order that we may better serve our fellow men.

That is the basic value of the book: to see beyond the spacial and cosmic presentation to the wellspring of compassion flowing from the heart of cosmos, to the galaxy, the solar system, our globe earth, to man. It is all a manifestation of a compassion beyond our ken.

FOREWORD

Mention must here be made of the tireless and painstaking efforts of every member of the editorial and printing staff: Kirby Van Mater, archivist; John P. Van Mater, who checked the manuscript prior to typesetting and prepared the Index; to Dorothy LeGros and Eloise Hart for the several typings required; to Madeline Clark, Manuel Oderberg, Ingrid Van Mater, Elsa-Brita Titchenell, Sarah B. Van Mater, and Lawrence Merkel, for the arduous task of proofreading; and not least, to the editorial committee, A. Studley Hart, the late Willy Ph. Felthuis, and Ida Postma, all of whom worked with me long and diligently to make this book a reality.

On this Centenary of Gottfried de Purucker's birth, we gratefully acknowledge our spiritual indebtedness to one who kindled anew the fires of aspiration, believing that FOUNTAIN-SOURCE OF OCCULTISM has power to inspire every earnest seeker for ages to come.

GRACE F. KNOCHE

January 15, 1974
Pasadena, California

Contents

Foreword / v

I — *The Primeval Wisdom-Teaching*
Passing on the Light / 3
Spiritual Illumination vs. Psychic Illusions / 8
The Still, Small Path / 14
Pledge-Fever and the Spiritual Will / 20

II — *Discipline precedes the Mysteries*
Esoteric Discipline / 29
Meditation and Yoga / 38
The Pāramitās and the Exalted Eightfold Path / 43
The Initiatory Cycle / 54

III — *Space and the Doctrine of Māyā*
The Void and the Fullness / 65
The Boundless in Ancient Cosmogonies / 70
Spaces of Space / 74
Space, Time and Duration / 79
Cosmic Reality and Mahāmāyā / 85
Parabrahman-Mūlaprakriti / 89
Manvantara: a Dream, a Māyā / 94
Hindu Conceptions of Māyā / 100
Spiritual Reality and Mind-Born Illusion / 105

CONTENTS

IV — *Galaxies and Solar Systems: their Genesis, Structure, and Destiny*

The Universe: a Living Organism / 111
Days and Nights of Brahmā / 114
Genesis of a Universal Solar System / 118
The Celestial Zodiac and the Birth of a Solar System / 125
Rāja Suns and the Cosmic Egg of Brahmā / 129
Reimbodiment of a Planetary Chain / 133
The Twelve Fohatic Magnetisms / 139
The Globe Zodiac / 143
Auric Egg: Cosmic and Microcosmic / 146
The Astro-Theogonical Aspect of the Cosmos / 149
Occult Physiological Structure of the Solar System / 153
Causative Nature of Cycles / 157
Cyclical Time Periods / 159
Racial Cycles and Yugas / 163

V — *Hierarchies and the Doctrine of Emanations*

Out of Paranirvana into Manvantara / 171
The Cosmic Spirit in Pralaya and Manvantara / 176
The Three Logoi / 182
Fohat, the Dynamic Energy of Cosmic Ideation / 189
On the Gnostic Aeons / 193
The Doctrine of Swabhāva / 198
Sound, Color and Number / 204
Architects and Builders / 209
The Lipikas / 216

VI — *Invisible Worlds and their Inhabitants*

Pattern of the World Structure / 223
The Unrolling of the Cosmic Elements / 227

CONTENTS

Elementals, Offspring of the Cosmic Elements / 232
Tattwas and the Seven Senses of Man / 238
The Birth of a Globe / 244
Planes and States of Consciousness / 250
Lokas and Talas / 256
The Human Life-Wave in the Loka-Talas / 261
Interwebbing of Lokas and Talas / 266
Monads, Centers of Consciousness / 270
The Monadic Classes / 277
The Triple Evolutionary Scheme / 283

VII — *The Doctrine of the Spheres*

The Heart of the Sun — a Divinity / 293
Sunspots and the Circulations of the Solar System / 299
Solar and Terrestrial Magnetism / 305
The Triadic Life of Father Sun / 309
The Twelve Sacred Planets / 317
Nature and Characteristics of the Planets / 326
Asteroids, Meteors, and Cosmic Dust / 337
The Moon / 340
The Planet of Death / 346
Life-Waves and the Inner Rounds / 350
Interplanetary and Interglobal Nirvana / 361
Śishtas and Manus / 369

VIII — *Gods — Monads — Life-Atoms*

Who are the Gods? / 379
Evolutionary Journey of the Monads / 383
Life-Atoms, their Origin and Destiny / 387
Heredity and the Life-Atoms / 394
The Doctrine of Transmigration / 398

The Cause of Disease / 403
Man is his own Karma / 410
Is Karma Ever Unmerited? / 415
Good and Evil / 421

IX — *Correlations of Cosmic and Human Constitutions*

The Auric Egg, its Nature and Function / 427
Monads, Egos and Souls / 432
The Auric Egg and Man's Principles / 439
Many Monads in Man / 446
Lost Souls and the Left-hand Path / 451
Occult Physiology / 458

X — *The Hierarchy of Compassion*

The Silent Watchers / 467
The Three Vestures / 474
The Dhyāni-chohanic Host / 477
The Avatāra — a Spiritual Event / 484
Upapādaka and Anupapādaka Avatāras / 487
Avatāras of Mahā-Vishnu and Mahā-Śiva / 492
Jesus the Avatāra / 495
The Power of Āveśa / 502
The Tibetan Lamaistic Hierarchy / 505
Fifth and Sixth Rounders / 512
Buddhas and Bodhisattvas / 517
Gautama the Buddha / 521
Our Spiritual Home / 529

XI — *Death and the Circulations of the Cosmos* — I

The Oneness of all Life / 535
The Causal Aspects of Death / 539

CONTENTS

The Process of Disimbodiment / 543
The Panoramic Vision / 549
The Prāṇas or Vital Essences / 555
Physical Death — an Electromagnetic Phenomenon / 560
Kāma-loka and the Second Death / 563
The Four States of Consciousness / 568
Ancient and Modern Spiritualism Contrasted / 574
The Nature of the Kāma-rūpa / 579

XII — *Death and the Circulations of the Cosmos* — II

Nature and Characteristics of the Devachan / 587
Length of the Devachanic Period / 593
Devachan and the Globes of the Planetary Chain / 599
Nirvana / 604
Sleep and Death are Brothers / 608
Through the Portals of Death / 615
The Process of Reimbodiment / 621
Inner and Outer Rounds / 627
Interplanetary Peregrinations / 632
Return Journey of the Reimbodying Ego / 637

Notes / 643

Appendices

The Precessional Cycle / 671
The Potency of Sound / 674
The Four Sacred Seasons / 678
H.P.B. / 680
Messengers from the Lodge — the Insignia Majestatis / 682
Nārada / 689

Index / 697